THE OFFICIAL

MP

MELROSE PLACE®
COMPANION

THE OFFICIAL

MELROSE PLACE®
COMPANION

BY DAVID WILD

WITH AN INTRODUCTION BY AARON SPELLING

HarperPerennial

A Division of HarperCollins*Publishers*

HarperCollins books may be purchased for educational, business, or sales promotional use. For information please write: Special Markets Department, HarperCollins Publishers, Inc., 10 East 53rd Street, New York, NY 10022.

FIRST EDITION

Designed by Charles Kreloff

Library of Congress Cataloging-in-Publication Data

Wild, David, 1961–
    The official Melrose Place companion / by David Wild. — 1st ed.
        p.   cm.
    ISBN 0-06-095147-8
    1. Melrose Place (Television program) I. Title
PN1992.77.M44W55   1995
791.45'72—dc20   95-21168

95 96 97 98 99 ❖/RRD10 9 8 7 6 5 4 3 2 1

Introduction

Melrose Place may not be my finest hours in television, but it has quite definitely given me some of my most fun hours.

Over the last three years, we have been fortunate enough to have a tremendous amount written about *Melrose Place* and all its popular characters. At times, though, it seems as if people forgot about all the fine folks who made the show such a truly extraordinary success. I'm speaking, of course, of the fantastic stars of the show as well as all the many unsung behind-the-scenes heroes responsible for putting together the show you love to watch each week.

Personally, I think it's wrong when people refer to the show as Aaron Spelling's *Melrose Place*. To me, the man

Mr. Television and producer of *Melrose Place*, Aaron Spelling.

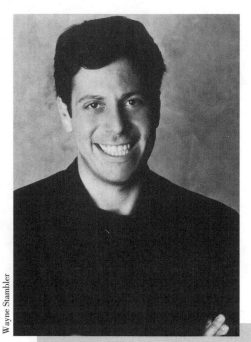

Wayne Stambler

Creator Darren Star.

who deserves more credit than he ever gets is Darren Star, the remarkably talented young man who created *Melrose Place* as well as *Beverly Hills, 90210.* Darren is a wonderful writer and, since almost the moment we first met at my house only four years ago, a very dear friend. Along with Darren, there is an extended family of writers, crew, and others whose dedicated and tireless efforts ultimately result in creating the weekly magic of *Melrose.* We're also fortunate to have the marvelous look of the show given to us by our other executive producer E. Duke Vincent.

Since we're fundamentally storytellers at Spelling Television, we felt it was only proper and fitting that we play a part in telling the story of *Melrose Place* as we see it. That's our reason for putting together *The Official Melrose Place Companion.* To help us with this project, we asked David Wild, who wrote a *Rolling Stone* cover story on the show that we all enjoyed greatly, to collaborate with us on a definitive *Melrose Place* book, one that captures the spirit and infectious fun that has marked the show.

This is, I believe, a story well worth telling. For all sorts of reasons, I am proud of the rise of *Melrose Place.* I'm gratified that *Melrose* has rather swiftly created a number of promising new young stars. And in the case of Heather Locklear—my own personal good luck charm—we've helped take an already established actress to a whole other level in her career.

Call our show bizarre, call it camp, or call it just good old-fashioned drama, the fact remains that *Melrose Place* is a remarkable success story. The residents of 4616 Melrose Place are now truly citizens of the world, familiar and beloved literally all around the globe. Anyone who's followed my career knows that I've been involved in a few splashy, sexy serial shows, for example, *Dynasty*, which was clearly skewed to an older generation than is *Melrose*. From the beginning, *Melrose* was a show geared toward a new generation. In fact, when I was first asked by my friends at Fox to get involved in young persons' shows like *90210* and *Melrose Place*, I felt that I was the wrong choice. Fortunately, time has proven me wrong, and for that I am very grateful. Believe me, doing TV series like *Beverly Hills, 90210* and *Melrose Place* can keep you feeling pretty young.

A number of the shows I've been associated with during my life in television have gone over the top, but at times *Melrose* has managed to go *over* over the top. God knows, when Kimberly took off her wig, we were beautifully way over the top. Much of the credit in this regard must go to those endlessly creative *Melrose* writers. It's been said that in television the writer is king, and the royally gifted *Melrose Place* writers under the vision of Darren Star and Frank South have never ceased to amaze me with their ability to come up with new thrills and story lines all the time. We have a saying on *Melrose* when someone comes up with a particularly wild idea: "You should be ashamed of yourself." Around here, it's usually meant as a great compliment.

In the end, though, I don't believe this bizarre, endlessly entertaining approach is the only explanation for the entire phenomenon of *Melrose Place*. There has always been something special about this particular show—something about it that connects not only with the young people to whom it was originally meant to appeal, but also with every sort of individual all over the planet. Boy, does *Melrose Place* connect. Some of the well-known individuals who've tuned into the show are quoted throughout *The Official Melrose Place Companion*. Unfortunately, discretion dictates that I don't reveal the names of some of the rather surprising *Melrose* fans I've come across. For instance, you would probably be stunned to hear about someone in an incredibly high position who's called me for a videotape of a *Melrose* episode because he and his wife went out and missed a show. This is a man who you'd imagine would think *60 Minutes* was light TV viewing. I remember getting calls from the head of a major film studio who was going on a cruise and desperately needed a *Melrose* videotape for the journey. Then there's a very big movie star who calls every week for his tape. And when he doesn't call, his wife does.

What drives all of us to *Melrose* mania? Phenomena such as this are always a bit of a mystery—otherwise all TV shows would be hits. My own guess is there's something else going on besides all the sexy stars and surprising subplots. Part of the powerful appeal of *Melrose Place* is that no matter what absolutely horrible things these characters say and do to each other every week, there somehow remains an odd but undeniable sense of bonding among them. Even our breakthrough villain Amanda has her vulnerable and very human side. Someone once asked me, "How can they all live at that place with all those crazy friends?" I said, "Ah, you've said the magic word." For all the madness of the show, these characters—and many of them are real characters—are friends. And that's what we all look for, I suppose.

If there's such a thing as a *Melrose Place* philosophy, I imagine that first and foremost it concerns living life to the fullest. That's something that Amanda, Alison, Jane, Jo, Sydney, Kimberly, Jake, Billy, Matt, and Michael most definitely do. Second, there's the sense that Thomas Wolfe was right—you can't go home again. The reality for most of us is that you really do have to rely on your new associates in your new surroundings in this life because your parents aren't always going to be there for you. Ultimately, we all have to come of age and make our own way in this world. And along the way, we all need a little help from our friends—no matter how crazy they may be.

As a father, I'm sorry to say that I think young people's problems in the world today are much more varied than ever before. Particularly in Los Angeles where *Melrose Place* is set and where so many of us involved with the show live, it sometimes feels like there's a calamity every day. There have been fires, floods, race riots, earthquakes. Perhaps the locusts are coming up next. The irony is that if we put all those things on *Melrose Place,* people would say, "Oh, come on." No one would buy it for a minute.

This is something I imagine the residents of 4616 Melrose Place have no doubt already learned about Los Angeles—one doesn't have to be crazy to live here, but it certainly helps.

—AARON SPELLING

A Fan's Notes

ecently I married the woman who introduced me to *Melrose Place.*

Next season, I hope to marry her sister.

My wife, Fran, is one of those brave and hardy television viewers who faithfully stayed with *Melrose Place* throughout all the growing pains of its promising but troubled first season. The two of us actually started dating during the start of the second season, and when she first opened up to me regarding her abounding affection for the show I must admit that I was initially rather skeptical. Within a few weeks, however, I had fallen—for the show, that is. Just a little later during that breakthrough second season I began to discover the true depths of my burgeoning passion for the show. My employer, *Rolling Stone,* had assigned me to cover a Paul McCartney tour of Argentina, and to my surprise, I found myself spending an inordinate amount of time and money on phone calls to Fran from Buenos Aires in a rather desperate long-distance attempt to get my weekly fix about what was going on in the most complex apartment complex in the world.

In short, I became utterly and rather happily hooked on *Melrose.* But fortunately—to quote John Lennon from "Imagine"—I'm not the only one.

When Judge Lance Ito asked the jurors for the O. J. Simpson trial to identify those television shows they simply "couldn't live without" while they were sequestered, *Melrose Place* made the list along with *60 Minutes*, football, and the Home Shopping Network. Around the same time, a study, released by a pizza-related trade organization, reported that delivery demand for that cheesy commodity escalated wildly during *Melrose* nights. The question remains, Why is it that the Simpson jury, all those pizza lovers, and I—as well as all the millions of other *Melrose* Heads out there—simply can't live without this show?

Certainly, I can't speak for those other good people. Indeed, even the reasons why *Melrose Place* connected so strongly with me remain something of a mystery. After all, I had somehow managed to go through three decades of moderately meaningful existence without so much as watching a single daytime or nighttime soap opera. To be brutally frank, in term's of favored television fare I had always been more of a *Twilight Zone/Nightline* kind of guy.

For many dedicated *Melrose Place* followers—some call themselves "Placemats"—the show possibly represents a sort of window into the sexy, semiglamorous world of young Los Angeles. For me, however, the show wasn't much of a leap into some faraway fantasy world. In fact, at the time I started watching *Melrose Place* I was living about a mile or so from Melrose Avenue, passing through that area's slightly tattered, self-consciously hip environs every morning on the way to work. The world of *Melrose Place* was quite literally a part of my daily commute. Like the more telegenic residents of 4616 Melrose Place, I was fortunate enough to live in the relative comfort of a groovy L.A. apartment. Tragically, however, my place cost more than theirs, and yet mine had no courtyard pool.

You could argue that what I found in *Melrose Place* was a Generation X–rated televised happening that says a lot—some might even say a tad too much—about these fast-and-furious post-MTV times. The slacker generation's down-and-dirty soap opera of choice, *Melrose Place* sometimes seems like the only place left in America where people are still having sex in the 1990s. Right away, the show seemed a revelation to me, someone who's spent years living in apartments without exchanging words—much less bodily fluids—with any of my own neighbors.

Indeed, *Melrose Place* may be the last spot in the country where there appears to be a true and enduring sense of community—however profoundly warped and twisted it may be. Not only does *Melrose Place* offer its residents a place where everybody knows your name, but more important, it's a wildly nonjudgmental place where everybody knows your game and still puts up with you anyway.

Possibly this helps explain why *Melrose Place* has become such a seductive and popular address. This is a remarkable show that offers its millions of viewers around the world in more than fifty countries a dreamy counterreality, a well-tanned utopia in which upwardly mobile ids roam freely, an oddly nurturing place in the heart where a woman can assume her ex-boyfriends will perish and a man can freely marry his wife's sister without fear of repercussions.

For the high-minded *Melrose* Head, the tortured and remarkably intertwined social lives of Amanda Woodward, Alison Parker, Billy Campbell, Jake Hanson, Jo Reynolds, Matt Fielding, Michael Mancini, Jane Mancini, Sydney Andrews, and Kimberly Shaw—as well as all the assorted psycho-love interests who pass through the world of *Melrose* at an astonishing clip—can prove far more gripping than the relatively uneventful nature of everyday existence. Think of *Melrose Place* as literate pop culture at its very best. Imagine *Ulysses: The Soap Opera*. Come to think of it, like Joyce's famed character Molly Bloom, the women of *Melrose Place* do tend to say "yes" a good deal. From a less literary, more sociological perspective, the show can be seen as an utterly inspired celebration of the joys of today's delayed adolescence—a prime-time bildungsroman for folks who are old enough to have already come of age at any other time in history.

Also the women are totally hot.

When Heather Locklear hosted *Saturday Night Live* in 1994, Wayne of *Wayne's World* managed to put his finger on this particular aspect of the show's appeal: "I am totally addicted to this show," quoth Wayne. "It's a babefest." One should note that by the end of the sketch Mike Meyers was wearing one of Amanda's sexy business suits.

To be honest, there's also no shortage of less high minded reasons for loving *Melrose Place*. The show's executive producer Aaron Spelling—Mr. Television himself who has earned a place in the *Guinness Book of World Records* for producing more hours of TV programming than anyone else—may be the man most qualified to understand the powerful appeal of the show. Spelling has called *Melrose* "some of my most fun hours." Clearly with his track record that's really saying something.

"In the beginning," *Melrose Place* and *Beverly Hills, 90210* creator Darren Star said in appropriately biblical terms, "our stories on *Melrose Place* were structured like the early *90210* shows with everybody learning moral lessons about life each show. But we discovered adults have absolutely no interest in watching other adults going through that sort of thing. They don't believe it. Now we try to write the show as fun, trashy, and compelling as we can. It's a delicate balance."

Before long, *Melrose* found that entertaining and profitable balance. And by the time some of the characters on *Melrose Place* started being sent away to various penal and mental institutions, the show itself was well on its way to becoming an institution in its own right.

Daphne Zuniga—who plays the much put-upon Jo Reynolds—has offered one insightful theory regarding the show's success. "Maybe *Melrose Place* is the thinking person's nighttime soap," she said. "You could say we're also equal-opportunity beefcake and cheesecake. If you like blonds, we've got blonds. You happen to want brunets, we've got brunets. And if you feel like a redhead, boy, do we have a redhead for you. We've got girls; we've got guys, too. We've got it all here at *Melrose Place*."

These days being a public Placemat is all the rage. In all aspects of our society from the White House to the typing pool, *Melrose Place* fans have made their feelings about the show known. In February 1995, *Seinfeld*—a show that runs on a competing network—featured a hilarious story line dealing with the pressing issue of *Melrose* addiction. In that memorable episode, a policewoman Jerry was attracted to strapped him into a lie detector machine to see if he was lying about not watching *Melrose Place*. Finally, of course, Jerry confessed to being a *Melrose* lover, as did George, Elaine, and even Kramer (who, incidentally, would make a great new pool boy for the *Melrose* complex). On *Ellen*, meanwhile, a stuffy intellectual love interest of the title character was deeply moved by his first *Melrose*. "Who is this gentle bard whose finger is on the pulse of all that makes us human?" he asks. "Aaron Spelling," Ellen tells him.

And it's not just fictional characters who love the show—Doug Savant who plays Matt Fielding reports that he ran into a huge *Melrose* fan by the name of John Wayne Bobbitt. More impressive, when popular talk show host Ricki Lake was arrested and put in jail overnight following an antifur protest in 1994, she was quoted as saying, "I made a big sacrifice. I missed my favorite show, *Melrose Place*." And when *Entertainment Weekly* asked White House power broker George Stephanopoulos if he watched the show, he said, "I'm usually working at that hour, but I get the tapes."

Obviously, *Melrose Place* lovers are literally everywhere. These days, the show's fans are even traveling down the fast lane of the information superhighway, spending quality time in various *Melrose* newsgroups on the Internet. And the phenomenon is clearly international. Not long ago Andrew Shue was shocked to discover that Israeli prime minister Yitzhak Rabin watches the show. Darren Star reports that *Melrose* mania was exploding full-force in Australia during his trip there. So to all the *Melrose* fans down under who are reading this: "G'day, mates, we'll throw another sultry subplot on the barbie for you."

Once upon a time it took a little guts for *Melrose Place* fans to stand by their show. My own *Melrose* moment of truth came when *Rolling Stone* asked me to write an article about the series *NYPD Blue*. Having never seen that show, I decided to take the opportunity to "out" myself to my editors. I begged them to have me cover a show about which I felt I had something to say. Thankfully, the fine folks at *Rolling Stone* saw fit to actually give me my dream assignment.

Getting to spend time on the set of my favorite show was, of course, a pleasure for me, although I did encounter a journalist's worst nightmare—there was no controversy, no major scandal, no big scenes going down in-between scenes. As Sally Field might have put it, these people liked each other; they really like each other.

"I've had shows in my career where it's really not a lot of fun to go visit the set," says Aaron Spelling with a laugh. "On *Melrose Place*, it's like one big party. In fact, it seems like Darren has always found a reason to throw a party every couple of minutes."

Appropriately enough, my resulting article ended up as a very popular cover story to *Rolling Stone*'s May 1994 "Hot Issue." The response to that story was truly remarkable. In nearly a decade with the magazine, I had never gotten so much overwhelmingly positive feedback on anything I had ever written. For *Place* lovers, this story seemed to come at some kind of watershed moment. By that time, *Melrose* Heads were already watching the show in support groups at private *Melrose Place* viewing parties everywhere. But here was someone daring to come out as a *Melrose* fan on newsstands everywhere. Taking my humble cue—I like to think—the silent majority of the show's fans came out of the woodwork with a truly Melrosian vengeance.

So it was then a genuine thrill when I got a call asking whether I would be interested in writing *The Official Melrose Place Companion.* In fact, it took me less time than a romantic entanglement on the show for me to say yes. After all, writers are always given the advice to write what they know and to write about what they love.

Speaking of love, my heart goes out to everyone who helped me get this book done under a tight schedule. In the film *Reality Bites,* Winona Ryder's character, Leiana, delivers the now-famous line *"Melrose Place* is a *really* good show." Many people contributed to this attempt to give that *really* good show a really good book.

Thanks go out to Aaron Spelling, Darren Star, E. Duke Vincent; the cast, crew, and great staff of *Melrose;* and Frank South, Chip Hayes, Kimberly Costello, Allison Robbins, Dee Johnson, Carol Mendelsohn, and Chuck Pratt. Instrumental in getting things done right were Debra Joester, Lisa Berlin, Renate Kamer, Cindy Napoli, Marnie Nir, Jennifer Hill, Dana Seely, Lisa Bell, Toni Moston, Genelle Izumi-Uyekawa, and Lisa San Miguel. The art of the deal was practiced with skill by my agent, Melanie Jackson, as well as by Angela Miller and Colleen O'Shea. My editor, Mauro DiPreta, arrived late in the game and proved to be a heroic figure of Jake-like proportions.

Thanks always to the entire Wild family, the Turk family, the Mersels, the Cotliars, Val Van Galder, Jack Farrell, David Rensin, and E. I am especially indebted to everyone at *Rolling Stone,* including Jann Wenner, Sid Holt, David Fricke, Karen Johnston,

Tom Conroy, Jancee Dunn, and Mark Coleman for their support regarding this project as well as for allowing me to quote from my own article.

And most of all, thanks are due to Fran, with whom every day is a *Melrose Place* party.

—DAVID WILD

THE OFFICIAL

MELROSE PLACE®
COMPANION

In the Beginning

*There is some soul of goodness in things evil, Would men
observingly distill it out.*
—William Shakespeare, *King Henry V,* IV.i

In the beginning, there was *Beverly Hills, 90210.* And as it is
written, *90210* begot *Melrose Place.*

History teaches us that the creation actually occurred sometime
back in 1990 when Darren Star—a savvy twenty-eight-year-old
screenwriter with big ideas but relatively modest credits like *Doing
Time on Planet Earth* and *If Looks Could Kill*—came to Fox to discuss doing a new show for the network. Star's own notion was to create a sort of "teensomething." This fine idea of matching angst and
actors of the acne-ages must have struck a resonant chord at the still
new fourth network. Apparently, Barry Diller, the head of Fox at that
time, had already considered doing a show set in Beverly Hills
High, and soon it was decided to try and put young Star together
with Aaron Spelling.

Spelling is a genuinely legendary figure in television. Having
produced close to three thousand hours of programming in his long
and famed career, Spelling has a truly remarkable list of credits that
starts with *Dick Powell's Zane Grey Theater* and continues at a rapid
pace through *The Mod Squad, Dynasty, Charlie's Angels, Family,*
and *And the Band Played On,* never seeming to end.

The original *Melrose Place* gang. *Clockwise from top:* Josie Bissett, Thomas Calabro, Andrew Shue, Courtney Thorne-Smith, Amy Locane, Grant Show, Doug Savant, and Vanessa Williams—as they begin the long climb up the staircase of success.

Andrew Semel

E. Duke Vincent—coexecutive producer of *Melrose Place* and Spelling's partner of eighteen years explains Spelling's place in television this way:

Courtesy of Spelling Television Inc.

Coexecutive producer E. Duke Vincent.

Aaron will go down in history as the most successful producer in the history of the medium. I don't think his record will ever be beat. In fact, Aaron is in the Guinness Book of World Records *as having his name on more television shows than anyone in history. And the guy who is second to him is me, because we've done so much together.*

"Aaron Spelling is God. No, really, think about it. Consider: Every period has its artists, its signal soul who single-handedly crystallizes the mark of everyday experience into a shining whole expression of that particular age, preserved intact for centuries to taste. Greece has its Homer, Renaissance Italy its Michaelangelo. John Steinbeck summed up Salinas Valley, Eudora Welty and William Faulkner fought the soul of the South, Tolstoy tackled Russia and Jane Austen re-created mannered England. Today, there's Aaron Spelling."
    —Shann Nix, *San Francisco Examiner Magazine*, 1994

Initially, however, Spelling admits to being a bit wary of getting involved with this new project. As Spelling told *Rolling Stone*'s Jay Martel in 1992, "My first reaction was 'Why me?' I hadn't done a young show since *Mod Squad*, for God's sake." As Spelling explains now:

> I got a call from Barry Diller about this high school show and I said I wasn't really interested. He said, 'Why don't you do it?' He thought that with my kids Randy and Tori, I should really be attuned to this. Then I got a call from Peter Chernin at Fox about Darren Star, and I saw a film he'd done. We met and talked at the house. I thought he was great and he was young and that he would certainly know the arena better than I would. And the rest—as they say—is history.

As Star recalls:

> They came up with a loose concept of doing a show about Beverly Hills, but they didn't know quite what to do. I never did television, but I knew the kind of show that I'd want to see. I'd never seen a show on television about teenagers that really reflected the way teenagers actually are. There were lots of movies that treated teenagers with respect—in fact, movies were generally geared toward teenagers. But there wasn't much of anything on television. Then the network put me together with Aaron Spelling and we got along famously. It was an extremely quick and relatively painless process.

As time would tell and dozens of shopping mall riots demonstrated, the idea of teaming Spelling's experience and Star's vision was an inspired and winning one. The show started its life as *Class of Beverly Hills*, a fish-out-of-water story about a family from Minneapolis that moved to the world's ritziest zip code. After the pilot, the show changed titles and focused increasingly on the kids of West Beverly. *Beverly Hills, 90210* slowly but surely became—and indeed remains—a full-out TV phenomenon. And so in the wonderful capitalistic world of network television, a resounding call rang out loud and clear for some sort of command repeat experience. According to Star:

> *I think not until the second season of* 90210 *were there rumblings about a spin-off. And* Melrose Place *was really a show I wanted to do anyway. I kind of convinced everyone that we could make this show a spin-off of* 90210. *I did not want to do a show about college because I always assumed—correctly as it turns out—that the* 90210 *characters would go on to college. I certainly didn't want to preempt that in any way. But I was anxious to write a show that dealt with adults, something closer to people my age, a show that my own peers would want to watch every week. If* 90210 *was teensomething, then* Melrose Place *was to be twentysomething.*

Rather than spinning off this new show from an existing character on *Melrose Place,* the idea was to place one of the future *Melrose Place* characters into the context of *Beverly Hills, 90210,* albeit relatively briefly.

And so it was that starting on April 30, 1992, and continuing on March 7, 1992, Jake Hanson—played with hunky conviction by Grant Show—appeared on two episodes of *Beverly Hills, 90210.* In the first of those episodes, "Mexican Standoff," Dylan McKay (Luke Perry) and Brenda Walsh (Shannen Doherty) are at the beach where Dylan's teaching his then main squeeze how to surf. Dylan then spots Jake riding into the parking lot. "Who is he?" Brenda reasonably asks of this macho vision in leather and denim. It turns out that Jake's the mystery man who taught Dylan how to surf, ride a motorcycle, and pick up girls. Apparently, Dylan thought Jake was living somewhere in the Pacific Northwest, but Jake explains he's now back in L.A. Then, most fortuitously, Dylan asks the big question:

Dylan:
So where you livin' these days, man?
Jake:
Ah, it's a little place off Melrose, nothing special.

> *"The original people at our parties were Julia Sweeney, me, Janeane Garofalo, and some other people from* The Ben Stiller Show. *Quentin Tarantino came. He couldn't really keep up the first*

5

time, he was a little overwhelmed. But I do remember one night when Quentin, Julia, and I watched a very special night with season-enders of 90210 and Melrose Place back to back, and Quentin seemed moved.

"The characters on Melrose have a great deal in their apartments, but they're all way too successful to live in there. They should all have big houses in Malibu by now. What's wrong with them? They're all in denial about how successful they are."

—Kathy Griffin, L.A. comedian who's thrown some of the most notable *Melrose Place* parties. The show has at times featured prominently in her act.

How wrong Jake would turn out to be.

Later in the same *90210* episode, Jake pops into the Peach Pit, where he's apparently an old favorite of the kindly proprietor, Nat. Asked what he does for a living by some of the younger *90210* characters, Jake is characteristically evasive. Soon though Kelly Taylor (Jennie Garth) has to go back home per her mother's request to pay the handy man who turns out to be Jake, who's been building Mrs. Taylor's wedding canopy in the backyard. Almost immediately there's significant chemistry between jailbait Kelly and the wood-working Jake, and Kelly starts wondering just how handy Jake really is. On Jake's way out that evening, their tasty flirtation heats up in the kitchen.

Kelly:
Listen, my mom's at Lamaze class, and I was just nuking some lasagna. If you're hungry, you could stay for dinner. If you're not busy.

Jake:
No, I'm not busy. I'm starved.

This being television, things escalate rather quickly:

Jake:
Smells great.

Kelly:
Yeah, I love lasagna.
Jake:
I'm not talking about the lasagna.

Before long, Kelly became totally smitten, provocatively asking her handy love interest if he needed "someone to hold your level." These kinds of construction come-ons make it clear that Kelly's infatuated.

By the March 7, 1992, follow-up episode, "Wedding Bell Blues," Jake and Kelly are kissing by the canopy. Sadly, Jake—being Jake—has begun to give her ill-explained reasons why she ought to stay away from him. "I'm the last person you should be bringing home to Mom," he tells her. In any case, this burgeoning love affair clearly annoys Kelly's old boyfriend Steve Sanders (Ian Ziering), a feeling he expresses with great subtlety:

Steve:
So how are things goin' with that guy . . . Joke?
Kelly:
Jake.

Bothered by the difference in their ages, Jake makes a passing attempt to stop Kelly from falling for him. Still the sexy talk continues unabated:

Jake:
I should probably be arrested for thinking what I'm thinking.
Kelly:
I won't call the cops.

By the end of this episode, all is well and Kelly and Jake can be seen making out at her mother's wedding reception.

The following fall, this ill-fated love affair carried over into the pilot for the new show named *Melrose Place*. The name of the series came quickly. "I wanted it centered around Melrose Avenue," recalls Star, who had worked in an office on Melrose for a few years.

"Melrose to me represents what's hip about L.A., even though in reality the area may have had its day to a degree. Somehow I thought it encapsulated that sort of twentysomething L.A." For the record, the actual Melrose Place is a small side street filled with a number of expensive antique stores.

According to Star, the notion for *Melrose Place* was—like its younger mothership series—rather personal and close to home for him:

> *90210 was sort of drawn in part from my memories of high school and from my impressions after having come out here for college of what it must have been like to go to high school here. And with* Melrose Place, *I had once lived in a building where it was like one step up from a fraternity house. Everybody was young and just starting out. Everybody had roommates, and yes, there was a pool. The funny thing is that we actually went to scout that building as a location for the show, and it was so ugly. I had all these fond memories of it, but in reality it looked like a Motel Six from the 1960s.*

With the pressure on for a spin-off phenomenon, the pilot was made rather swiftly. As Star remembers:

> *The show came together incredibly fast. At the time I was supervising 90210. I was also writing the pilot for* Melrose Place, *and I didn't finish it until January, and the show was on the air in July with a full-series order. Which meant that by the time the first episode was on the air, we already had a few more in the can and six shows written. It was all very fast. And I think that's one reason the show had some growing pains at the start.*

"After a long day, I want to be entertained. I watch it religiously. I actually discuss Melrose on Thursdays with a journalist who covers the Pentagon."
—A high-placed Pentagon official, quoted in *Rolling Stone*, 1994

Before those pains came the crucial matter of casting the show and putting together a production team to bring it to life. The audition process for *Melrose Place* was somewhat complicated by the fact that Spelling and Star weren't the only ones targeting a youthful demographic market around this time. The hotly contested Generation X–rated sweepstakes of 1992 saw young America offered an absurdly full slate of postadolescent programming. This is easy to forget now since *The Heights* took a fall, *Class of '96* dropped out, *2000 Malibu Road* was condemned, and *The Round Table* got put away in permanent storage. But at the time all that tubular youthful activity meant that there was a rush for the young and telegenic.

But as Star explains:

> Melrose *got a jump start on casting because we got a green light before those other shows did. So we had the pick of the litter. The casting of* Melrose *was all the more a daunting task after having cast* 90210, *a show that created a lot of new stars. That was a tall order to live up to. I feel like we're very, very lucky to have the cast that we have, because there were all those other shows like* The Round Table *and* The Heights *that didn't last. I'm sure they had good casts too. But now I can't imagine anyone else in these roles. I think we made the right decisions and that's one place where having Aaron Spelling on the team really comes in handy. He has an extraordinary eye for casting.*

Grant Show—who'd left the daytime soap *Ryan's Hope* to study at the London Academy of Music and Dramatic Arts—signed on first to play Jake Hanson, the show's strong, silent-type transition man from *90210*. Courtney Thorne-Smith, who'd appeared in the films *Lucas* and *Summer School* and who had played a Laker Girl on *L.A. Law*, was selected to be aspiring ad woman Alison Parker. New York theater actor Thomas Calabro—who'd been a regular in the short-lived series *Dream Street*—was chosen to play Dr. Michael Mancini. Josie Bissett, a successful model who appeared on a number of television shows including *The Hogan Family*, got her job as Jane Mancini, the then-good doctor's wife. Doug

Savant—who had appeared on *Knots Landing* and in a number of feature films—was cast as social worker Matt Fielding. Vanessa Williams—a New York theater actress not to be confused with the well-known singer of the same name—came aboard as Rhonda Blair, teacher of cardiofunk at the Aerobicision Health & Fitness Center. Young film actress Amy Locane (*Cry-Baby, School Ties*) was chosen to play Sandy Harling, the southern-fried Shooters waitress and wannabe thespian.

The last to join the original *Melrose* cast was Andrew Shue. In fact, another young actor had been chosen to play aspiring writer Billy Campbell, but shortly after shooting the pilot began, the decision was made to recast. Shue—the younger brother of actress Elizabeth Shue (*Cocktail, Adventures in Babysitting*)—had just done another series pilot for Spelling that wouldn't be picked up. At the very last minute—actually a few minutes after the very last minute—Shue stepped right into the role.

As Shue says, "The other show I thought was going to happen didn't, and Aaron told me he wanted me to read for *Melrose* instead. I believe I auditioned on a Saturday and was working on *Melrose* on Monday."

Aaron Spelling calls Shue's last-minute entrance "the great story of casting *Melrose*." As he recalls:

> We cast a Canadian actor, and his readings were marvelous. But during rehearsals the director told me to keep looking. We shot one day and fortunately it was a Thursday. We saw the dailies on Friday. By Saturday morning we had thirty-two actors at my house sitting in my projector room while we were in my office reading them. There were the folks from Fox as well as Darren and I. They all agreed on an actor, a very good actor, who I thought was completely the wrong choice. He was such a heavy, that I couldn't see Alison letting him in the apartment, much less being roommates with him. Then Andrew read, but everyone decided to go with another actor. I don't often get mad, but I was frustrated and walked out of the room. Peter Chernin from Fox came out and said, "Who do you want to play Billy?" I said, "Andrew Shue." Peter replied, "If you feel that strongly, let's do it." It was that close.

Also signing onto the original team were other key players like the show's line producer, Chip Hayes, whose importance Star feels ought never be underestimated. "We hand Chip and his people the script, and say, 'Now, go shoot it,' and they make it happen." Hayes was already something of a Spelling veteran, as he says:

Courtesy of Spelling Television Inc.

Line producer Chip Hayes.

I started during summers off from school in the mailroom when Aaron was doing The Mod Squad *and* The Rookies. *After school, I joined him as a production assistant on* Fantasy Island *for a few years. Then I moved myself up to associate producer on shows like* T. J. Hooker *and a justifiably unknown show called* The Bad Cats, *which was significant only because we had Michelle Pfeiffer in it. Next I went over to the network and wore a suit for ABC, until I came back to Spelling. Then E. Duke Vincent told me he had a few new pilots for me and the one I happened to land on was* Melrose Place. *It was definitely the right one to land on.*

Early publicity for *Melrose Place* centered necessarily on Show since his high-profile *90210* appearances meant that he was *Melrose*'s first face forward. He even managed to make the cover of *People* before *Melrose* debuted. As Show recalls:

I knew that I wasn't really the pivot man for Melrose Place. *I was just the easiest target. It was easiest to attach everything to my face in the beginning because the others hadn't even been cast. Andrew wasn't cast until two days into shooting. But I knew this was clearly an ensemble show.* Melrose Place *was definitely never intended as Jake's show.*

On July 8, 1992, *Melrose Place* debuted on the Fox network at 9:00 P.M., immediately following *Beverly Hills, 90210. Melrose* premiered during summer repeat doldrums to give the show a head start on the upcoming fall series. The show's highly desirable time slot placement ensured that *Melrose* could be seen by an audience that was at least one hour older and more sophisticated than the *90210* crowd. And in a vivid further display of Spelling-Star synergy, the first three episodes featured the rapid spluttering out of the Jake-Kelly relationship, with the tough but good-hearted Jake ultimately deciding to throw the little one back for her own good. Along the way, the spinning-off process continued with *90210* cast members Tori Spelling, Ian Ziering, and Brian Austin Green even stopping by for a nonalcoholic beverage at *Melrose Place*'s beloved hangout Shooters.

"I had dinner with Darren Star years ago because he wanted me to write an episode of Beverly Hills, 90210. That didn't work out because I wanted to do a show in which everyone got killed. I figured it could be a special Halloween episode. But in the beginning I probably watched Melrose because I did enjoy watching 90210, and it was easier than turning the TV off. Most people started paying attention because everyone on the show is so good-looking. But then they started spicing Melrose up. And now all sorts of people I know—I'm talking about lawyers and other authors—really get into it. They began talking about these characters as if they actually existed. Does the show say anything about Generation X? Undoubtedly. Do I have to say what that is? It's a fantasy version of ourselves. That's probably the same thing that made Peyton Place so appealing to another generation."

—Bret Easton Ellis, author of *Less Than Zero* and *American Psycho*

In retrospect, Star thinks the spin-off—though it served a purpose—was not entirely well spun:

I think the big mistake was thinking of it as a spin-off at all. The reality was there was not much of a relationship between the two shows. Melrose Place—had it been developed a little more independently of 90210—might have gotten where we wanted it a little sooner. We carried a lot of baggage from 90210 in terms of storytelling and perception. That bogged the show down at the beginning, especially the first twelve or so episodes. Eventually, though, we got where we should be.

Spelling—who admits to being a tad worried about the show's future during the first five or six episodes—explains that a television series taking some time to find itself is nothing new:

Often things don't happen quickly. For example, things didn't really kick in for Dynasty *until the third season. With* Melrose *we learned from our mistakes. Early on, the whole show would be like—Billy moves in. When we started, the episodes had to have an ending. We couldn't have a two-parter. Now we do eight-parters. I do remember Darren and I meeting one day, and I said, "Why don't we just go for it." And thanks to Darren, we certainly have!*

To the true *Melrose Place* scholar, the troubled but promising first season represents a sort of televised Rosetta Stone, full of many coded hints of things to come. Time-shifting through the first season can prove an odd, if moving, experience. Seeing the good Dr. Mancini—a future heavyweight champion troublemaker—coping with the building's plumbing problems and somehow managing to keep his own misbehavior under control through much of the season is fascinating and almost poignant. To watch Matt Fielding share such a close friendship with Rhonda knowing full well that she will move on before long is heartbreaking. Hearing Sandy's deep-fried southern accent come and go with the wind is, quite frankly, simply baffling.

Perhaps the most shocking thing about the first season of *Melrose Place* was all the endless bonding among the gang at 4616 Melrose. Early on, the apartment courtyard literally overflowed with prodigious supplies of friendship and good cheer. They swam together, ate together, jogged together, barbecued together, played poker together, watched ball games together, and went to abortion clinics together. Hell, some of them even *bungee jumped* together. One curious exception: They didn't sleep together much—not even those newly married Mancinis.

By the end of the first season, some voice of commercially-minded reason had clearly cried out, "Can't we all *not* get along?" But in those early days of *Melrose Place*, these residents didn't simply reside in the same building—they formed a sort of attractive live-in support group for one another. No matter what minor dramas were dealt with during each episode—and many of them were quite minor—by show's end the residents of Melrose Place were usually jumping in the pool together. As Grant Show recalls, "It was just a different show. We missed the mark, I think. The shows in the first season would be about Jake going back to get his college diploma. Like who gives a shit? People want to see people being bad to one another. There was no tension. No conflict. We really were a bunch of saps the first season."

Castmate Courtney Thorne-Smith—who spent much of her first season as Alison Parker not sleeping with Billy Campbell—concurs. "We were just eight good kids trying to make it. As a sitcom, that might have been great, but we were supposed to be a drama. Then Amanda and Sydney arrived and created conflict. Now you can root for the good guys and still get off on all the bad guys at the same time."

Andrew Shue—who speedily built a female fan base in his role as Billy—credits the changing pace of the plots that the writers started coming up with:

> *These days we have four or more story lines going at once. When we started out it was like the early 90210, each episode had an issue it dealt with, and then it had to be wrapped up somehow by the end of the show. That method is good for reruns, but it wasn't so great for a show. These days a whole lot of stuff is always happening. And there's really no doubt what our audience wants to see—relationships. They really want to see the interaction, the competition, and*

the divisions between these people. And that's what we give them.

Early ratings for *Melrose Place* were disappointing—read "lousy"—and reviews generally weren't much better. "It's like each apartment at Melrose Place came with a free lobotomy and a gift certificate from the Gap," wrote Greg Dawson of the *Orlando Sentinel.* Some cast members worried about cancellation. Still, Show explained in 1994 that one of *Melrose*'s obvious liquid assets gave him confidence that the show would be around for a good long while:

Timothy White

The Mancinis go shopping in more carefree days.

Actually, the minute I walked onto the set of the show and saw that they'd built a real swimming pool, I had this feeling that we'd be around for a while. Forget about actors, man, pools aren't cheap. But I also think that pool was part of the whole Brady Bunch *attitude of the show that gave us trouble in the beginning. You know—everyone was nice and everything ended happily. And the pool was there so we could all gather at the end of the episode to have a barbecue and be hunky dory. These days we couldn't get together in the pool because someone would probably end up drowning someone else.*

There was little doubt among all concerned parties early on in the first season that some changes had to be instituted to make *Melrose Place* less of a bottom dweller in the ratings department. As Star recalls:

A show really has to find itself, and it seemed to take us a year to separate ourselves from 90210. Most shows benefit from being a spin-off, but the connection kind of hamstrung us actually. I think it was really around episode twelve when Alison starts to have her affair with Keith that the characters really started acting like adults, and things began to turn around. But the truth is that there were many dark moments. I believe early on Amy Locane compared being on the show to being on the Titanic.

Fortunately, from the beginning, *Melrose Place* had some powerful and well-placed supporters such as Fox executives Dan McDermott and Bob Greenblatt. As McDermott, executive vice president of current programming and specials, recalls:

The ratings were very disappointing, but at the network we never really considered canceling the show for a number of reasons. First, we knew that ultimately the combination of Darren's tremendous young talent and Aaron's incomparable experience was just unbeatable. There was mutual respect and love there. When you have a team like that, and they're open to working with the network to explore what it takes to make the show work, you stay with it even if it's ninetieth in the ratings. Then there was the practical matter that we had nothing else ready to put on Wednesdays at nine P.M. Also, based on our 90210 experience we knew that if the show's working creatively, we'll find a way to bring in an audience. And when Darren and Aaron torqued things up, the show just took off.

"What I like about the show is it's California oriented. Living in the East and being an academic, I'm around nerdy people who are hypercritical of efforts at sustained excellence. To me, southern California is gorgeous people who are totally supportive of superficial efforts at mediocrity. I watch and think, 'God, wouldn't it be nice to have a constituency like that?'"
—Clifford Winston, senior fellow at the Brookings Institution, explaining his interest in the show, quoted in *Rolling Stone,* 1994

Eventually all sorts of changes were made. The first cast departure came when Sandy, and thus Amy Locane, left the show after the thirteenth episode (titled "Dreams Come True"). As only the most obsessive *Melrose* Head will remember, Sandy moved to New York to play the role of sexy young neurosurgeon, Aviva Lester, on the daytime soap opera *Forever and Tomorrow.* One could only ponder who would take Sandy's favorite place poolside, a vantage point from which she could warn women away from knocking on Jake's door. For his part, Show is quick to defend Locane, saying it wasn't the actress's fault that her character didn't make the cut. "With Amy, one episode they'd want her to have a heavy accent," he says, "the next no accent. Everyone screwed with the character so much that eventually they just couldn't salvage it."

As it turned out, there really wasn't much time to miss Sandy. Only two episodes later Jo Reynolds moved into the building. In her first episode, "House of God," Jo came across as an abrasive, pushy New Yorker. Before long, Jo revealed herself as the good-hearted wannabe photographer fleeing an abusive marriage whom we've all come to know and love.

According to *Melrose* writer Chuck Pratt, Jr.—who went on to become executive producer of *Models inc.*—bringing on the character of Jo was indicative of the searching going on behind the scenes between Star and key writers like himself and Frank South: "We were sort of casting about trying to see what worked. Billy and Alison just worked for us. I think we originally brought in Jo in hopes that she would be for us what

The lovely Amy Locane as Sandy.

Timothy White

Hope from *thirtysomething* was for that series. That didn't really work, but we knew we had a great character and actress who'd stick around anyway."

Star chose Daphne Zuniga to play Jo. Zuniga was a talented film actress perhaps best known at that point for her starring role opposite John Cusack in Rob Reiner's 1985 hit romantic comedy *The Sure Thing*. Coincidentally, Zuniga was one of Star's roommates back in college at UCLA. As Star says:

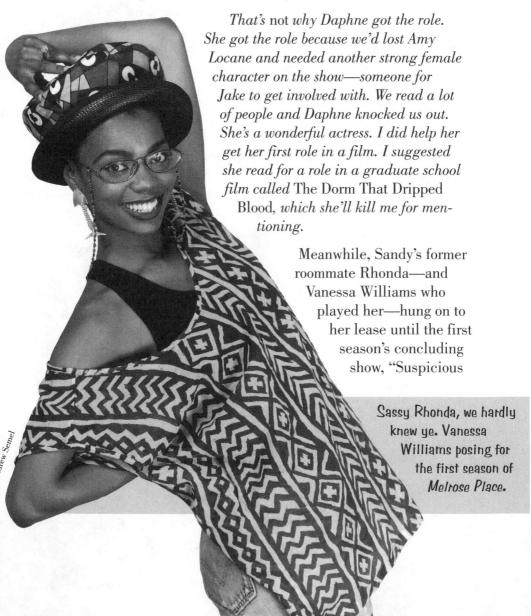

That's not *why Daphne got the role. She got the role because we'd lost Amy Locane and needed another strong female character on the show—someone for Jake to get involved with. We read a lot of people and Daphne knocked us out. She's a wonderful actress. I did help her get her first role in a film. I suggested she read for a role in a graduate school film called* The Dorm That Dripped Blood, *which she'll kill me for mentioning.*

Meanwhile, Sandy's former roommate Rhonda—and Vanessa Williams who played her—hung on to her lease until the first season's concluding show, "Suspicious

Sassy Rhonda, we hardly knew ye. Vanessa Williams posing for the first season of *Melrose Place*.

Andrew Semel

Minds." At the end of that two-hour episode, Rhonda seemed set to head off into the sunset with her husband-to-be Terrence. She has never returned. Of these sudden departures, Star recalls:

> *It's always tough to tell someone you're not keeping them on. But I think any good actor—and both of these women were good—wouldn't want to be a part of an ensemble show in which their characters were not working. Their scenes just weren't working out. It wasn't their fault. Maybe the actress character Sandy could have worked, but with Rhonda, I don't think anybody cared about the day-to-day life of an aerobics instructor. I think possibly that was just a little too shallow.*

Fittingly enough, one of those most worried about Rhonda's end-of-season departure was Doug Savant, who played her supportive buddy Matt. As Savant said, "Matt had nothing to do that first season. I'd just go, 'Yes, Rhonda,' 'Good, Rhonda,' 'Go get 'em, Rhonda.' And I'd beg for anything to do on the show. But I really just ended up supporting Rhonda and encouraging Rhonda. So when Rhonda left the show I was very worried. I was like, 'Help me Rhonda.'"

Fortunately, by this time, help had already arrived at *Melrose Place* in the shapely form of perhaps the sexiest bitch in all of television history.

What's in a Name

Alas, the average viewer doesn't usually get to see them, but the creators of *Melrose Place* nonetheless take the time to title each episode of the show. And, as the show has gotten increasingly witty over the seasons, so too have the titles. Often these titles make allusions to famed works of the past. Except for the occasional clunker like "Peanut Butter and Jealousy" and some episodes that sound vaguely like adult entertainment—such as "Hot and Bothered" and "Arousing Suspicion"—these Melrose titles are all quite good really. Here then, in the interest of full disclosure, is a totally subjective list of the top ten *Melrose Place* titles to date.

Timothy White

10. "Of Bikes and Men."

An episode from the second season of *Melrose Place* in which, in addition to so many other things, Jake tastes the grapes of wrath following the emotional loss of his shop, Jake's Bikes.

9. "Devil with the G-String On."

Melrose goes Mitch Ryder one better in this second-season episode that included Sydney's memorable, minimalist appearance at Billy's bachelor party.

8. "It's a Bad World After All."

This rather dark and non-Disney-tinged episode from the third season of *Melrose Place* deals with Alison trying once and for all to confront her sexually abusive father.

7. "I Am Curious, Melrose."

Like the later episode "The Cook, the Creep, His Lover and Her Sister," the title of this third season opener, in which Alison and her sister, Meridith, confront their twisted father, reveals a strong art house streak.

n Ragel

Diego Uchitel

6. "Hose by Any Other Name."

This rather elegant phrase was used to sum up the episode in which Mancini Design appears to accidentally become partners with the mob in selling pantyhose and drugs.

5. "Love, Mancini Style."

Here's a title that celebrates the full all-in-the-family romance of the not-so-good doctor.

4. "In-Laws and Outlaws."

Another celebration of family in this episode from the third season that saw Jo doing battle with Reed's parents, the Carters.

3. "The Bitch Is Back."

No, not a show with a special guest appearance by Elton John, but rather the dramatic episode from the second season in which Kimberly comes back from the near dead.

Doug Hyun

2. "Much Ado About Everything."

Even Shakespeare himself didn't cram as much action into one play as was jammed into this extraordinarily packed second-season opener in which—among so much else—Keith stalks his beloved Alison.

And the number one best *Melrose Place* title of all time:

1. "They Shoot Mothers Don't They?"

There are no horses in this tense episode that sees new mom Jo get shot by Reed's parents.

And God Created Amanda

Though she be but little, she is fierce.
—William Shakespeare, *A Midsummer Night's Dream*, III.ii

W hen Heather Locklear first appeared as Amanda Woodward on the twenty-first episode of *Melrose Place*—"Picture Imperfect," which aired on January 27, 1993—she was billed as

Doug Hyun

A typically tense moment between Alison and Amanda during "Irreconcilable Similarities."

making a special guest appearance. By the very next episode, "Three's a Crowd," Amanda was already making her full-court press move on Billy and almost instantly alienating her colleague Alison in the process. The original plan called for Locklear—already a familiar attractive face from her concurrent roles as Sammy Jo on *Dynasty* and Stacey on *T. J. Hooker*—to appear on *Melrose Place* for four episodes, with an option for two more should things work out. Nearly three years and some seventy-five episodes later, Locklear remains *Melrose Place*'s valued special guest star for life. As Locklear recalls:

> *I think I first knew I'd be sticking around for a while when the fourth episode came and I was still there making waves, still causing trouble. Pretty soon I was missing the next TV pilot season because I was working on* Melrose, *and that turned out to be a pretty good thing. With all the intertwining plot lines, I guess it just got harder and harder for them to get rid of me.*

Not that anyone had any reason to want to get rid of Amanda. Almost instantly—in its more sordid and salacious post-Amanda era—*Melrose Place* began to turn around and draw more and more viewers to the series during the latter part of the first season. As the season drew to a close, things got increasingly soapy in the very best sense of the word. As Star remembers:

> *Heather brought us a villainess that was lacking on the show. We were beginning to develop Michael into a villain, but we did not have a villainess, and Amanda gave us one hell of one. She also served to be the catalyst to bring Billy and Alison together, which was really important. By falling for Billy, Amanda made Alison realize that she in fact was in love with him. That set up the love triangle that we didn't have before. I also think Heather's name brought a lot of people back to the show to see what she was doing right at a time when the show was really working. I give her a lot of credit for that.*

The bitchy edge that the character of Amanda brought to the show clearly struck a chord with viewers. And why not? She is truly a bitch among bitches. Aaron Spelling sees Amanda as part of a very well established tradition. As he's said:

> It's like what I once said about Joan Collins's character Alexis. A snake always has the best lines. And if you don't believe me, go back and read how much dialogue Adam and Eve had. The bitchy part always has the best lines. And I think they really wrote Amanda brilliantly. What they've done with her—which we didn't do enough with Joan's character—is give her a strange sort of vulnerability.

In a highly profitable display of the theory that one bad apple spoils the whole bunch, Amanda set off a rather powerful and strange chemical reaction in the *Melrose Place* complex. All of a sudden, in this bastion of goodwill and love for thy neighbor, assorted bad guys and girls started popping up *everywhere*. "Everybody had just been too good before," says Josie Bissett who plays Jane Mancini, "Everything was too easy. We were all such good friends in the beginning. Then we fixed that and got some sexual tension going, and things started working *much* better."

> "Melrose Place *is like* 90210 *without parents, so there's no conscience on the show. The best thing about the show? Heather Locklear! I watched her in* Dynasty. *I watch her in* Melrose."
> —Jack Moline, rabbi at Temple Acudas Achim in Alexandria, Virginia, quoted in *Rolling Stone,* 1994

By the twenty-seventh episode, "Pushing Boundaries," which aired on March 24, 1993, Michael Mancini was pushing his mouth onto that of willing colleague, Kimberly Shaw, kicking off one of the most speedy and sustained moral declines in recent memory. Joining Mike in hell was the lovely Sydney Andrews, Jane's screwy but lovable kid sister, vividly played with all-American charm gone wrong by newcomer Laura Leighton. Sydney first graced *Melrose Place* with her presence in the middle of the first season in "Single White Sister." By the very next episode, "Peanut Butter and Jealousy," Jane was having a bad dream in which Sydney and Michael were having an affair. By the time of the thirty-ninth episode early in the second season—"Flirting with Disaster," which aired on October 20, 1993—Jane's worst nightmare had come true.

Interestingly, the rise of Syd resulted in one of the only apparent factual contradictions in the show's history. In an early episode, Jane had alluded to being an only child. "We didn't know what the hell to do about that," Aaron Spelling says with a laugh. "Maybe she meant that she was the only child that her parents cared about."

The pace of the show picked up exponentially—indeed almost everything changed. And for their part, the cast took to the changes readily. "The whole thing evolved nicely," says Thomas Calabro, whose character Dr. Michael Mancini certainly underwent the most dramatic transition. With his tongue at least partially in cheek, he's said:

> *I think what happened is that the writers were getting to know us. I'll never live that one down! Actually, I think it was just the natural process of the piece finding its own voice, as my wife likes to say. When they saw what was happening between Michael and Kimberly, they ran with it. Originally we were this staid couple that people in the building came to for advice. Not a lot of drama in that.*

Faster than a speeding rock video, the show started to spike each and every episode with enough sex, drugs, and rock 'n' roll that if one blinked, one was bound to miss a significant romantic relationship. Sanity-challenged *Melrose* love interests like Alison's ecopsycho Keith and Jo's Reed added the element of danger to everyday life at 4616 Melrose Place. Sydney returned with a vengeance, breaking at least ten of the seven deadly sins along the way, bottoming out at least temporarily when she went to work for Lauren, a Heidi Fleiss–like Hollywood madam. Dr. Mancini earned his doctorate in screwing up the lives of everyone around him. Even Matt made a splash with a "don't ask, don't tell, don't kiss on camera" romance with Jeffrey, a gay naval officer.

According to writer Frank South—now *Melrose*'s coexecutive producer—the idea was to venture into the realm of the timely and the outrageous while still having the show maintain its own internal logic: "There has to be some sort of gut-level logic to it, a certain *Melrose* reality about it for us. We really don't do alien abductions."

"Melrose Place *is the source from which my deepest emotional thirst is quenched. Without it, I die!*"
—Jill Goodacre Connick, fashion model, married to musician Harry Connick, Jr.

Coproducer Kimberly Costello, another writer, agrees that "there's got to be some seed of reality there for the show to work for us and for the viewer." According to story editor Dee Johnson, even as seemingly wild a decision as Sydney's stint in the world's oldest profession was justified. "Sydney joining the hookers came from a place that made sense," Johnson explains. "They needed her and she needed to be needed at that time." Executive story editor Allison Robbins believes that, ironically, the character of Amanda brought much more than short skirts and lots of attitude to the show. "I really think that in a strange way, Amanda brought reality to the show," says Robbins. "She added the competition in the workplace and elsewhere, and just brought things up several notches."

The same cannot be said of Locklear. Other cast members quickly got over any fear of Locklear, a more established star, coming in and upsetting their cozy ensemble. As Show recalls, "There was no big territorial thing. But, personally, just knowing who Heather was, I figured this woman is going to be a diva, and she's going to ruin the whole gig. Fortunately, I was dead wrong. Heather's great and totally fun to work with."

That feeling was most definitely mutual. As Locklear remembers:

> *They'd had a lot of people coming through the show, so I'm not sure that they cared about me coming in. I mean why should they? Andrew was probably like five years old when I was first on TV. So I'm sure it was like, Who's she? I had a great time. On all my other shows I was the youngest one, the low man on the totem pole. So this felt great. If I were seventy, maybe I'd be wishing I were playing a twenty-year-old. But*

for now it was great to play my own age and be the slightly older woman.

Locklear says that in addition to having more fun hanging around with actors closer to her own age, this demographic move resulted in her finding a whole new audience. She says, "The shows I've done like *Dynasty* and *T. J. Hooker* were geared to an older audience, so for a while there the younger population really had no idea who I was. Now kids in high school and even elementary school know who I am, which is a lot of fun."

> "There's always been some excuse: I don't have time. One person can't make a difference. I'd miss Melrose Place."
> —Ellen Degeneres, listing excuses for not doing the right thing on *Ellen*, 1994

Locklear wasn't the only one having fun. Indeed, as the second season of *Melrose Place* continued on outrageously, the show gradually started to explode in the ratings, despite airing opposite perhaps the most popular comedy series on the air, *Home Improvement.* As Spelling recalls:

It was amazing because both Melrose Place *and* Beverly Hills, 90210 *were in serious trouble at different points. But I can't tell you of any show I've been connected with that exploded like* Melrose *did. I mean, yes,* Charlie's Angels *exploded, but for totally different reasons, as we all know. We had three of the most beautiful ladies in the world who worked for a man over the phone and made five hundred a week and wore five-thousand-dollar Nolan Miller gowns, so you know why that show took off. But I can remember being very pleasantly excited because when* Melrose *hit, it hit very big.*

Soon the show was not just making better ratings, it was becoming a topic of conversation—both in the media and around water-coolers everywhere. Reflecting the appeal of the show and its youthful demographic, the stars of the series began popping up both inside and on the cover of just about every sort of publication. Locklear's face in particular was turning up with great regularity at all levels of the media food chain. And though many observers were quick to credit her with turning *Melrose*'s fortunes around, Locklear was fast to point out she was simply part of a winning team. As she said in 1994:

> *Yesterday morning, I was driving to work half-asleep, listening to Howard Stern when I hear this ad for* Inside Edition *announcing, "Tonight, Heather Locklear's private videos" or something. So now I'm getting sorta nervous, thinking who the hell sold them my home videos? So I watch, and it turns out to be this totally complimentary piece about how I came in and saved both* Dynasty *and* Melrose *during the second season. Unfortunately, they failed to mention that Joan Collins also came on [*Dynasty*] that season, which might have had something to do with it. Believe me, with* Melrose *there's lots of people who deserve credit. I'm just happy to be here.*

Darren Star—a fellow with some experience running TV shows with explosive sets—says that the *Melrose* set developed organically into a professional, productive place:

> *Honestly, people get along very well. That's great, because with all the work, I don't know how people would survive otherwise. As much as the media loves to report on controversy on these sets, you don't hear that about* Melrose. *We had a great, respectful group of actors going in. I think it probably also helped to be around Heather, someone who deals with her celebrity with such grace. Maybe she sets a certain standard of behavior.*

Throughout 1994, the behavior of the *Melrose Place* cast—imaginary or otherwise—became of more and more interest to the general public. Word leaked out that Thorne-Smith and Shue were a real-life item during the first season. Late in the second season, similar talk would emerge about Leighton and Show. Rumors spread, including one rather curious one that Shue was leaving to return to play soccer in Zimbabwe, where he'd played after graduating Dartmouth. As Shue said in 1994:

> *You don't sense the mania walking around, but it's there. We don't get mobbed like the 90210 people do, so it's easier to forget that the whole country is watching us. That rumor got started because there was some blurb in Us magazine in which I talked about going back to Zimbabwe for a couple of weeks to play with my old team during hiatus. Some people misunderstood that, and all of a sudden there are people everywhere concerned that I'm not coming back, which is kind of amazing.*

The *Melrose* actors all dealt with this success and newfound attention in their own ways. Shue, for example, decided to use his national platform to create Do Something!—a national youth community service program. Not that the actors really had much time for outside activities. This is partly the result of *Melrose Place* producing many more episodes than the average series. The second season had thirty episodes, and since then an additional two episodes have been tacked on to the network's order each season. As a result, *Melrose Place* has revolutionized the exhausting art of what's known as "double-ups"—a complicated process by which at certain points in the season two episodes of an ensemble show are filmed at the exact same time. As Chip Hayes explains with a tired laugh:

> *The real insanity didn't begin until the second season. Doing two episodes at once in "double-ups" is something we've really pioneered. By now we've sort of built it into our system. For us, it's still seven days per episode, only we do two episodes in that same seven days. Every time a script comes in, Harry Bring—the unit production manager—and I break it down on his computer. And when we're in "double-ups," we break the actors into two teams—the blue and the red. And it really becomes like putting together a jigsaw puzzle to make it all work.*

> "*I think I understand what makes* Melrose Place *work for me. I know people in that age group and they're quiet, nice peo-*

ple. *Bad things don't happen to them each week. Oh, sure, things happen every now and again, but it's a rather mundane existence. Someone should be experiencing all this life. So that's what* Melrose *does for us—we can live vicariously and dangerously. I don't know anyone with a big scar on her head. I don't know anyone who leans into a mirror, takes her wig off and says, 'Half my skull is gone.' So for me it's nice to be able to turn it on and see a woman who's around the age of women I know, and yet she's got an enormous scar. And she's evil. It's very rare that I say, 'I know that woman, and she's pure evil.'* Melrose *is like a catastrophic* thirtysomething. *On* thirtysome-thing *you'd have to actually watch the person go through the disease. On* Melrose, *they get through the whole thing in a week. And the next week they're fine and the next week they're having a baby. Hey, give me tragedy, but give it to me quick."*
—Jon Stewart, stand-up comedian and host of
The Jon Stewart Show

Indeed, from a production point of view, *Melrose Place* is a remarkable undertaking, demanding a daunting amount from the show's crew of between fifty and sixty people. As E. Duke Vincent explains:

> *This is a very ambitious process. We do try to give the audience a feature film–quality type show in an hour form. Nobody tries to do that and does thirty-two or more hours a season. We're exhausting everyone concerned. But the crews we have are so finely tuned. They are literally the absolute best in the business. There's no one out there better—in my opinion—and that includes feature film crews.* Melrose Place *is as expensive as any of the hours on television, but we don't cheat. We put it on the screen.*

By the end of its breakthrough second season, *Melrose Place* had turned the corner, and then some. The show was hitting its stride both from a creative and ratings sense. Darren Star and others on the show were happy that just about everything they tried was working. As Star recalls:

We'd come a long way from the first season when there was no shortage of things not working. Even though some people may think of Melrose Place *as mindless entertainment, we started discovering that when we want to we can get something in there that's controversial and provocative.*

Occasionally, there were frustrations, such as when the network refused to show Matt's on-screen kiss with Billy's best man, Rob, in the season-closing "Till Death Do Us Part." Mostly, though, *Melrose Place* went as far as its imaginative creators desired. Indeed, throughout the whole second season, the show bravely pushed the envelop dramatically. As Frank South recalls, "We were really testing the waters. I kind of felt like I had to leave the country last year before the two-hour season finale went on the air because I thought people would think it was just outrageous, with Kimberly plotting to kill Michael and Alison facing down her father."

Fortunately, the audience response was resoundingly positive. As Allison Robbins puts it, "Anything we thought was too out there, we soon discovered worked anyway."

Ten *Melrose Place* Episodes That Shook the World

Such is the embarrassment of Melrosian riches that it would be virtually impossible to select the ten best episodes of *Melrose Place* thus far. Instead, submitted for your approval, are ten *Melrose*s that had maximum impact on the show and on the world at large. They are listed in chronological order.

1. "Single White Sister."
There are many ways to pinpoint *Melrose*'s dramatic turn to the dark and funny side, but certainly one came with this first-season show that marked the arrival of Jane's twisted sister, Syd.

2. "My New Partner."
There is a brief shining moment here when Alison and newcomer Amanda Woodward look like they're going to be the best of friends. Fortunately, this never came to pass.

3. "Carpe Diem."
Alison and Billy finally seize the day and one another in Palm Springs and make love for the first time in this climactic episode. Jane has less fun, walking in on Michael and Kimberly.

Andrew Semel

4. "Suspicious Minds."
This conclusion to the first season was a jam-packed ninety-minute episode that saw Jane face down Kimberly, Rhonda propose to Terrence and—most pivotal—Amanda buy the whole damn building.

5. "Revenge."
Though it's always sad to bid a psychopath like Keith adieu, this was a key episode that proved that, in defense of his beloved Alison, Billy could be sensitive *and* tough.

Doug Hyun

6. "Otherwise Engaged."
Is there anything prettier than a beautiful bride? Yes, as it turns out—in this case, it's two lovely but contentious sisters getting into a watery battle over just one wedding dress.

7. "The Bitch Is Back."
Was there ever such a near-death experience so creepy and so much darn fun for the whole family than that of Kimberly Shaw? This is the episode that saw Kim take her famous scar-revealing trip to the bathroom—the grunge generation's equivalent of Janet Leigh's *Psycho* shower scene.

8. "Till Death Do Us Part."
What could be better than two hours of *Melrose*? Whereas other shows would build up to a marriage, only *Melrose Place* would crescendo with a nonwedding, namely Alison's and Billy's near nuptials. All this plus incest and Matt kissing the best man.

9. "Just Say No."

Viva Las Vegas! In the most hysterical, action-packed hijacking in all of television history, Aussie creep Chris forces Syd to have a decadent blast in a luxurious suite at Caesar's Palace. And for lover's of sweet revenge, the temporarily unestranged Jane got to use Michael for a change.

Doug Hyun

Doug Hyun

10. "The Big Bang Theory."

Talk about knowing how to go out with a bang, this two-hour episode saw *Melrose* end its third season in high style. Betrayals, a wedding—and the only thing separating the apartment complex from an explosive ending was an alternative personality—it doesn't get any better than this.

The Show Must Go On

To do a great right, do a little wrong.
—William Shakespeare, *The Merchant of Venice*, IV.i

"**M**ondays Are a Bitch."

With that memorable ad line and an especially seductive photo of Heather Locklear, *Melrose Place* promoted its risky but ultimately successful move to a brand new location for the 1994–95 season. Inside Fox, the decision was made to take its prized new phenomenon—now in its third season—and attempt to build a new Monday night of programming around it. As Aaron Spelling recalls:

> *At that point the interest in* Melrose Place *had gotten so intense that it was getting pretty crazy. There were screaming phone calls and angry letters because people arranged their schedule around the show. They thought we ruined their whole night, because now they couldn't see* Melrose *and* 90210 *together. That "Mondays Are a Bitch" campaign was one of the greatest posters I've ever seen. I thought maybe Heather would go crazy. A lot of people wouldn't have a sense of humor and might have objected. But Heather's so amazing, she just thought the whole thing was a kick. And fortunately we got great ratings and demographics in a very rough time, and it was great to not be up against* Home Improvement. *In the end, we beat everything Fox ever had on Monday nights. We're thrilled it's worked out.*

Diego Uchitel

According to the Fox network's Dan McDermott, this move to Mondays reflected the network's strong faith in *Melrose*: "It was a difficult choice. But the network was growing, just as it's still growing, and when you're trying to build a new night for a network you have got to go with your strongest stuff, an anchor show that brings people in. We were sorry to lose that two-hour block, but it was a necessity."

Initially, replacing *Melrose Place* as the new follow-up show to *Beverly Hills, 90210* was *Models inc.* In what was now becoming something of a Spelling tradition, *Models inc.* became a sort of semi-spin-off from *Melrose Place*. Appropriately enough, this spin-off was very much a dysfunctional family affair. Amanda's long-lost, and to be honest, long-resented mother, Hillary, returned toward the end of the second season in the form of former *Dallas* diva Linda Gray in the episode charmingly titled "The Bitch Is Back." As it played out, Jo Reynolds was doing a beach photo shoot with a group of models, including Sarah Owens, played by Cassidy Rae. Amanda appears and forces Jo to fire Sarah because she's from Models inc., an agency with which she emphatically and mysteriously refuses to do business. Before long we figure out the true reason—not-so-dear not-so-old Mom is the CEO of Models inc.

Over the course of three episodes, Hillary and Amanda bond badly—it certainly doesn't help matters when Hillary's dastardly boyfriend, Chas Russell, sues Amanda for sexual harassment. Ultimately, this mother and child reunion was not to be an extended one—just long enough to kick start *Models inc.* as a summer-replacement series. Darren Star chose not to become involved with *Models inc.*, but *Melrose*'s Chuck Pratt moved over to serve as the new show's executive producer. As Pratt says now:

> *After the amazing second season at* Melrose, *I think I forgot what first seasons can be like with a show that's trying to find itself. And so for me the first season of* Models *has been in some ways like a flashback. Sometimes I'll talk to Darren or Frank South about things that go on and say, "Remember dealing with this." And they'll look at me a little blankly. I think that maybe they've blocked it out for psychological reasons—probably they're hoping they'll never have to repeat it. Unfortunately, a lot of times that learning process is inevitable.*

And though Amanda and her mom seem destined to be less than close, these two Fox network foxes would eventually at least share Monday evenings on the same channel.

"They've pulled off something quite amazing on Melrose. Having acted and directed for the show, I've realized there's a fine line between pushing the envelope dramatically and taking things too far. The story lines on Melrose Place are really out there, but they manage to stop just short of turning off the audi-

Courtesy of Spelling Television Inc.

ence. *The way the scenes are set, the dialogue is written, and the cast plays it all, they make everything fun, yet still give it just enough reality to keep the audience with them. They're on a real tightrope there. And the cast has gotten their chops down fast. Having been there myself, I can say that I was a much slower learner."*
—Parker Stevenson, a TV veteran who once starred in *The Hardy Boys* and who played Alison's high-tech love interest during the second season of *Melrose.* He has also directed episodes of *Melrose Place* and *Models Inc.*

Meanwhile, back at *Melrose Place*, things continued to hop along at a remarkable pace, right from the season debut, "I Am Curious, Melrose." That episode was directed by Charles Correll, a member of the talented team of revolving directors that have become part of the extended *Melrose* family. Though there's not time around the *Melrose Place* set even to consider dozens of takes of each scene, much less explore all aspects of the *auteur* theory, these directors clearly make a major contribution to the success of the show. As Chip Hayes puts it:

> *When you're doing as many episodes as we do, you try to find directors that will give you a good show, but also who the cast will enjoy working with and who will make the process as creative and easy as possible. They've got to inject a lot of creativity without creating too much angst for everyone around them. And over the years, we found a few people whom we like to stick with—people like Charlie Correll, Richard Lang, and Chip Chalmers (who started out as our assistant director). Victoria Hochberg came in the first year and impressed us, and she's come back and done a number of shows, as has Jefferson Kibbee. That's the core group, and then there are people*

39

we bring in occasionally, such as Parker Stevenson who did some very nice jobs for us after he guest starred on the show.

On-screen things picked up even more during the third season. As Fox's Dan McDermott observes:

The convention of the soap opera was always to drag things out for as long as possible. A single story could take six months. Darren decided to do it in one episode. That style of storytelling is unique in prime-time series. No one tells a story as quickly and yet as completely as he does. He gives the audience a lot of credit for being able to assimilate a lot of story at a quick pace. That's why no one gets bored watching the show.

"It's pretty clear how the show changed between the first season and the other two seasons," says Laura Leighton. "The tone became admittedly camp. It finally fessed up and became what it is wholeheartedly and enthusiastically."

Behind the scenes, the show hit its stride. According to most accounts, the show was ever becoming a well-oiled machine. As Chip Hayes says:

Knock on wood, we've been lucky. I have worked on shows where there's one actor who has problems, and that kind of person can make their problems into everyone else's problems. This cast is the best. At first I thought it wouldn't last—just wait till they get a little success—but it never happened. I wish I had some dirt for you. Life really doesn't imitate Melrose around here. And it seems like the more nefarious the character, the sweeter the actor. Everyone asks "Is Heather Locklear really a bitch?" And she's the furthest thing in the world from that. They all pull together and get the job done.

> "The great thing about Melrose Place is that you can not see it for months, and then flip it on and get immediately sucked in all over again."
> —Kathy Valentine, bassist for the Go-Gos, a notable girl group, popular years before Melrose Place's Bod Squad made the scene

Fox remains anxious to show as much *Melrose* as it possibly can. As Aaron Spelling says:

> *For the third season, we're doing thirty-two episodes, and for the fourth, we're doing thirty-four. My God, that's a lot of hours. I will never forget a meeting I once had with Rupert Murdoch's office. He asked if we could do forty episodes a year. I had to explain that would probably mean shooting seven days a week all year. As it is, everyone makes a remarkable effort. It wasn't my idea to do thirty-four next year. I called Frank South and his group and said "Can you do thirty-two?" And they said, "We can do thirty-four." So of course, I called Fox up and told them, and they said, "Great, you want to do thirty-six?"*

Melrose Place was becoming not only a productive machine but a profitable one as well. Helping out the bottom line of producing an expensive show like *Melrose Place* was the fact that more and more merchandise began to hit the market. Now you didn't have to watch the show—you could listen to it and wear it. *Melrose Place—The Music* released in 1994 by Giant Records is a winning sample of alternative rock artists including Paul Westerberg, Sam Phillips, Urge Overkill, Annie Lennox, and Divinyls. Two songs from the album—Aimee Mann's "That's Just What You Are" and Letters to Cleo's "Here & Now"—have already become major hits on alternative radio. There's also a full line of *Melrose* T-shirts, hats, sweatshirts, and other wearable memorabilia. Still to come is *Melrose* perfume, a scent that will no doubt redefine the sweet smell of success. Certainly, there's much more to come. "We've thought of making a Dr. Mancini doll," Spelling joked to *Rolling Stone*, "but we didn't know where he'd put the stethoscope!"

There's even talk—I hear—of *Melrose Place* books.

> "The characters and plots on Melrose Place remind us there is never a dull moment in Los Angeles."
> —Richard Riordan, mayor of Los Angeles

At the center of all this activity and big business remains the show itself.

Frank South—who's been a key player creatively since the middle of the show's first season—will take over as executive producer of *Melrose Place* for the 1995–96 season. Working under his guidance will be the crack team of writers whom Star and Spelling both call some of the show's greatest unsung heroes: coproducer Kimberly Costello, executive story editor Allison Robbins, story editor Dee Johnson, and supervising producer Carol Mendelsohn.

South and Star seem to be of one mind when it comes to the timeless message of *Melrose Place*. As Star says, "Generation X is a very convenient media slogan, and I'm glad that *Melrose* is supposedly the choice of this generation. But I think our basic themes are universal and timeless: People are looking for love and trying to find themselves, and work at jobs where they get along with their bosses."

Or, alternatively, as South puts it:

> *What we're saying to this generation or any generation is to attack life with a passion. No one on our show sits around, so they're not slackers. These days when you see someone hanging around the pool you wonder why they're not somewhere defusing a bomb. They all do go after life with gusto. We're not deep at* Melrose, *but if we're saying anything it's that it is difficult out there these days—a tough place to make a living or have a relationship. On* Melrose Place, *you're lucky just to make it through the day alive.*

According to Fox's Dan McDermott, the show remains in very good hands: "Darren's as talented a guy as there is, and so, of course, it's hard professionally and personally to see him move on to other things. But fortunately, Frank and his writers are just amazing. I think Darren's left behind a team that knows how to make *Melrose* work and work well. I'm happy to say I can see this show going on for a long time."

As Spelling put it, "We're going to miss Darren without a doubt. It has been a marvelous collaboration. But Frank South has really just blossomed and I think we're all going to be just fine."

E. Duke Vincent is similarly optimistic:

As long as you keep introducing new characters to the show—and witness what we've already done on 90210—there is no real outside limit. You can blue-sky almost any scenario that you want. New personalities emerge and begin to drive the arcs of a story. And when they do, we'll take the hint. Obviously, you have your main anchor characters that you want to keep as long as possible. But how long can this show go on? Well, you tell me?

So how long can it go on? Here's what Darren Star has to say on the subject: "I think the show can last as long as the writing stays sharp and exciting, and the actors stay with it. Who knows? The great thing is it's an apartment complex, so people can move in, move out, and move back in."

Ultimately, no one—not even Aaron Spelling—really knows how long the fun can last. But here's one hint. When I mentioned to Spelling the fact that there does just happen to be one retirement home right in the middle of the real-life Melrose area, I do believe I saw a light bulb go on over his head.

Heather Locklear:
Q & A

It takes a lovely lady to play as enormous a bitch as Amanda Woodward, and certainly there can be no doubt that in the world of *Melrose Place,* Heather Locklear *is* that lovely lady. Femme fatales don't come any more adorable and businesslike than Amanda. Locklear—who Aaron Spelling very affectionately calls "my good luck charm"—made a huge splash in the 1980s starring on *Dynasty* and *T. J. Hooker* simultaneously. Since that time, she's appeared in numerous miniseries and TV movies and the occasional feature film. Locklear's *Melrose* colleagues all uniformly credit her with setting a standard of professionalism on the set and helping turn the show's fortunes around. Immediately, she was embraced as the youngest older woman in history. As the devilish yet oddly vulnerable Amanda, Locklear was able to bring the show to new levels of moral degradation. She may also have single-handedly—or should that be double-leggedly?—revolutionized the very concept of appropriate office wear. Of such things are great TV shows made. Whatever the hell she's selling at D&D, we're buying it. Inquiring rock 'n' rollers may want to note that Amanda's favorite album of all time, *Stranger in This Town,* just happens to be the solo effort of Richie Sambora, Bon Jovi's well-married guitarist.

What's the biggest difference between you and Amanda?

She's an incredible bitch.

What do you think Amanda brought to the show?

Short skirts and a sharp tongue.

45

Any theories on why the characters don't use the pool much anymore?

We're all over thirty. No, no, that's just me. Maybe it's not heated anymore.

Does life imitate Melrose Place*?*

I hope not.

Do you miss all the bonding of the characters from the first season?

Amanda never bonded with anyone.

Have you ever attended a Melrose-*watching party?*

Only my own. There was lots of champagne, lots of gossip—watching and not listening.

What do you think Amanda's rent is?

Free, free, free.

What couple that hasn't happened on the show yet would you most like to see?

I think that Matt and Kimberly would be very interesting!

Do you think Alison and Billy will ever get married? Should they?

I think that every season should have a Billy and Alison cliffhanger wedding where they never get married.

To Billy's chagrin, Amanda takes a phone call from her dad in "Bye-Bye, Billy."

Doug Hyun

What factors made Melrose Place succeed while so many other twentysomething shows failed?

Aaron Spelling.

What three adjectives best describe Amanda?

Ambitious, self-serving, and misunderstood (Ha!).

What do you imagine is Amanda's favorite album?

Stranger in This Town.

How come we haven't seen the laundry room much lately?

We all have house cleaners now who do the laundry.

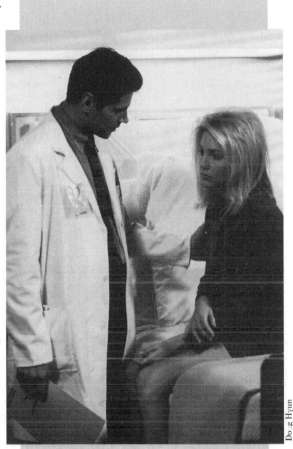

The not-so-good Dr. Mancini comforts Amanda after her cancer diagnosis.

What's your favorite line of dialogue you've spoken on the show?

"You bastard!"

What's your least favorite?

The monologues I have to give at D&D about which I know nothing.

What departed Melrose Place character would you most like to see pay a return visit?

Nasty Peter Burns.

Amanda and Jake share a quiet moment.

Wayne Stambler

How did Amanda get so tough?

I figure she learned everything from her dad.

What are the questions that fans ask you the most?

In the beginning they told me to leave Billy and Alison alone. Now they ask, "Why are you so mean to Alison?" and "Is Billy really that cute?"

What do you think Amanda thinks of Sydney?

Actually, Amanda kinda likes Syd. She admires her for getting away with so much. She's an Amanda in training. Actually, she's worse.

What bothers her so much about Alison?

Amanda's a professional. She sees Alison as a little incompetent.

So is it a matter of love-hate or just hate-hate?

There's no love. It's all pretty surface and fake for both of us. I love the way it always goes back to, "Well, thanks for being a friend." They always pull that one on each other. Actually, Amanda does that more to Alison.

Any favorite Amanda outfits?

They are all short and tight. Only the color changes.

What kind of projects have you squeezed in during Melrose *breaks?*

Saturday Night Live, Texas Justice, and lots of photo shoots.

How has the show changed over these three seasons?

The story lines keep getting more outrageous.

What reaction did you get when Amanda got cancer?

People worry Amanda's going to get nice because she got ill. I tell them she won't, and they seem relieved.

Who from the real world would you like to see move into Melrose Place?

With Alison's ouster complete, Amanda and Brooke celebrate.

Doug Hyun

My friend Juliet Walsh, 'cause she's dying to be on TV.

One of the writers on the show, Alison Robbins, says that in a funny way Amanda brought some reality to the show.

Amanda and reality? Now, that's scary.

How would you sum up the Melrose Place *philosophy?*

Shut up and lay down.

"There's a great chemistry between all the characters—you can tell they get into it. Everybody I run into seems to like the show. I think the guys love to watch it for all the good-looking women on the show. And, of course, all the ladies love it. Amanda—I mean, Heather—tells me it's a lot of fun being a bitch, a side of her personality that I never see. And obviously she's really great at it."
—Richie Sambora, Bon Jovi guitarist, who enjoys watching the show with his wife, Heather Locklear

"Like most adult beauties, she claims to have been an ugly kid: skinny, bad teeth, and acne so severe she implored God to intervene."
—Rob Tannenbaum, profiling Heather Locklear in *Details*, 1994

Ladies and Gentlemen, Welcome to the First Annual Mandy Awards

Named in honor of Amanda Woodward's dreaded childhood nickname, "Mandy," the Mandy Awards are presented to honor Special Melrosian Achievement in a variety of categories. As on the show, speeches are to be kept to a bare minimum so that more fun stuff can happen.

The Robert Shapiro Award for Promoting the Law on a Hit TV Series

And the winner is . . . Walter Kovacs, one of the very best attorneys in the Melrose area who bailed Jo out of a mess following the whole Reed murder fiasco. One wonders why she hired Adam Waxman—played by veteran actor John Saxon—for her custody case. Could it be because Waxman looks a little bit like Bob Shapiro?

The Rabbi Harold Kushner Award for the Character Who Most Continually Demonstrates What Happens When Bad Things Happen to Good People

And the winner is . . . Jobeth Reynolds, for living a remarkably Job-like existence with rare grace and style. Men, if you are dysfunctional, don't worry, Jo will get around to you eventually. If not, there's always Jane or Alison.

The Chuck Manson Award for Inexplicably Twisted and Degenerate Behavior by a Supporting Player

And the winner is . . . Chris Marchette. While certainly there are legions of scary freakazoids on *Melrose Place* who, it could be argued, deserve this extremely prestigious prize, Jane Mancini's sexually perverted swindler of a boyfriend takes the trophy home because he managed to be utterly evil, and he did it with a really cheesy Australian accent.

The Alan Alda Award for Telegenic Male Sensitivity by a Male Lead in a Prime-Time Series

And the winner is . . . Billy Campbell, the very evolved fellow for putting up with tremendous amounts of sustained romantic torture from Alison Parker while still managing to "miss" her through much of it.

The Amy Vanderbilt Award for Outstanding Civil Behavior in an Ethically Shaky Apartment Complex

And the winner is . . . Matt Fielding for managing to maintain his moral standards while all around him frolic freely in the muck and mire of *Melrose*.

The Lee Iacocca Award for a Special Guest Star Promoting the Cause of American Industry

And the winner is . . . Amanda Woodward who's dogged professionalism proves that one need not act warm and fuzzy to be one hell of a boss.

The Heidi Fleiss Award for High Profile Promiscuity in Prime Time

And the winner is . . . Sydney Andrews for her groundbreaking and, frankly, exciting work in bringing a certain indefinable, all-American, oddly wholesome quality to sluttiness.

The Dan Quayle Citation for the Presentation of Family Values in Prime Time

And the winner is . . . the Mancinis. Forget about Murphy Brown, the Mancinis are a true family for the 1990s. Sure, Jane and Michael may be divorced, but they keep the connection alive and she has kept the name.

The Tammy Wynette Prize for Standing by One's Man for More Than One Season

And the winner is . . . Kimberly Shaw, for her remarkable and refreshing dedication to Michael Mancini even following her decision to kill him.

The Dale Carnegie Award for Professional Advancement in an Ensemble Drama

And the winner is . . . Alison Parker, for her inspiring rise from receptionist to president of D&D in just under three seasons.

The Joycelyn Elders Prize for the Celebration of Human Sexuality in Prime Time

And the winner is . . . Jake Hanson, who has maintained his good guy image while gradually and systematically having his way with virtually every woman who enters the building.

Andrew Shue: Q & A

Billy Campbell moved into 4616 Melrose Place in the pilot episode of the show, and he's been moving *Melrose* watchers, particularly female watchers ever since. Starting as a slightly cocky but lovable Valley guy, Billy's transformed into a gifted magazine journalist, then a promising young ad man. Mostly, though, he's been a steadfastly sensitive and earnest boy toy. For many long-time viewers, Billy's relationship with Alison has often been the heart and soul of the show. It was also over Billy that Alison and Amanda first kicked off their historically entertaining series of clashes. The last of the original ensemble to be cast, Andrew Shue was an early breakout star from the show, despite having been acting professionally for just over a year at the time. Shue credits his sister Elizabeth Shue

In "Long Night's Journey," Billy takes a dip in the overheated pool.

(*Cocktail, Adventures in Babysitting*) with giving him some early pointers. Deciding to do something positive with his newfound fame, Andrew cofounded Do Something! (in 1994)—a national organization run by young people that assists young leaders in building communities across the nation.

Who's the most surprising Melrose Place *fan you've encountered?*

The prime minister of Israel.

Are you serious?

Yeah, I was at a luncheon honoring him, and it turned out that I was invited because the prime minister and his wife watch *Melrose Place*. I had a little goatee at the time and I hadn't shaved in a week, and he came up to me, touched my beard, and said, "Oh, I like you on TV, but I don't remember this." I left there thinking that I was in the *Twilight Zone*.

Does it excite or concern you that people in position of world power watch Melrose?

It's understandable that everybody wants some kind of fantasy world and release from their everyday life. President Clinton wants to watch basketball on the weekend, you know, something to watch and relax. *Melrose Place* fills that void for some people.

So do you think Billy and Alison will end up getting married?

Based on what we've seen so far, I figure Alison and Billy will end up coming back together in some sense. Something always brings them back together. Not necessarily romantically, but in some sense. They're in the same world all the time, so I think it'll probably happen. But who knows?

Do you think it would be a good idea?

I think you better talk to the writers about that one.

Does life ever imitate Melrose Place?

Sometimes, yeah, especially in this town. When you hear the kind of struggles people have here and all the back stabbing that goes on, it can get pretty *Melrose* at times. You have people coming to this town from all sorts of different kinds of worlds trying to get somewhere fast. That makes it a strange place. If you think about it, the characters on *Melrose* are a very odd group.

Andrew Shue catches a pass on the set of "Irreconcilable Similarities."

Doug Hyu

One big dysfunctional family?

I think that's the way a lot of L.A. is. Really.

Do you have a favorite Melrose *episode?*

There've been a lot of great ones as far as the whole cast is concerned. For me, the one I enjoyed doing the most was the one in which Billy's father died. The whole episode was basically about that story. I put a lot of work into that one.

Billy and Brooke—forever?

Doug Hyun

Any least favorite?

Early on in the first season there was an episode where within one episode I meet a girl, end up liking her, bring her home to the apartment, she moves in for three days, we say we love each other. By the end of the show, I'd broken up with her and everything's fine again. All in one episode.

Any theories about why no one goes in the pool much anymore?

We do a lot less of all group activities these days.

Do you think the show says anything about Generation X?

I think the whole Generation X thing is kind of silly. But there's no doubt that if you want you could generalize by saying these people are often confused by what they want to do. There's no doubt that young people today are searching for more. There's not a clear, set path to follow. So it's no surprise that the people on *Melrose Place* are all over the place.

What couple that hasn't happened yet would you like to see in the future?

Matt and Michael. Maybe Kimberly and Jane.

How has Melrose *changed your life?*

Most everybody else had been acting for a good while. I'd only been acting a year when I got the show. This is my first real part. I had no experience. It's definitely changed my life in a major way.

Obviously, your Do Something! foundation has taken a lot of your free time. Do you have time for other outside projects?

I have a deal with Joel Silver to do a film next hiatus.

And Do Something! is very much ongoing?

Absolutely. It's a lifetime commitment.

So what do you figure Billy's favorite album would be?

Billy's definitely a guy who likes to hear the words. I think he likes Tom Petty and the Heartbreakers and Bruce Springsteen.

Is there anyone from the real world you would like to see move into Melrose Place?

O. J. Simpson would be pretty interesting, and I've heard that he actually likes the show.

Courtney Thorne-Smith: Q & A

"**A** dysfunctional Mary Tyler Moore for the 1990s," is how Darren Star envisioned the character Alison Parker—though there are varying theories regarding the degree to which Alison is dysfunctional. From the start, Alison has proven to be an extremely pivotal character in the success story of *Melrose Place.* Right away, the slow-burning story line of romance among roommates Alison and Billy captured the viewing public's imagination. A little later, the

Jon Ragel

wonderfully vindictive office cat fighting at D&D Advertising between Alison and Amanda helped goose the show to tremendous ratings. Considering her youth, Courtney Thorne-Smith was already

Jon Ragel

a seasoned actress by the time she joined *Melrose,* having appeared in feature films such as *Lucas, Summer School,* and *Revenge of the Nerds II,* as well as playing a memorably seductive young Laker Girl on the television series *L.A. Law.*

What romance that hasn't happened yet on Melrose Place *would you like to see?*

It's going to have to be Alison and Amanda soon.

So you figure that those two have a love-hate thing going on?

It's got to be a love-hate thing or we just wouldn't talk to one another. We're all so grotesquely bound together. I was talking to Daphne about that recently because we were having another situation in which Alison does something horrible to Jo, her pal, just out of being careless and self-centered. And again, Jo says, "It's okay, I understand that you were going through a hard time." I do these horrible things—I lose her child for her, and I get her fired, and it's okay because I don't mean to.

So what keeps these people together?

Who knows? I was watching with my boyfriend last week, and Amanda was in her apartment, and he said, "Let me get this straight. She's the president of a major advertising company and she lives in a one-bedroom apartment in a courtyard building?" I said, "That's right."

How much do you figure Alison's paying for rent these days?

I would guess eight hundred. It seems to be a sliding scale, so it can be afforded by a waitress or a president of a company. It's communism as practiced only in *Melrose Place.*

An important sexual history question here: In the first season, Alison and Jake had a very brief fling, but how far

Alison and Billy: their on-off-on-and-off-again relationship keeps going and going. . . .

Diego Uchitel

Jon Ragel

they went is unclear. Did they actually do it?

We still debate that. It's funny because this is where the lines get a little blurry. Andrew says, "No way. No way you two did it." And I think it's a little unclear because in my head we didn't, but when we play the scene that takes place the next morning it was way sexier than I planned on playing it. I didn't mean to. We finished and I said, "Oh, I just had sex, didn't I."

Do you think Alison and Billy will get married?

I think they're annoying together. I think they're whiny and self-centered. But my interpretation of how soap operas work is that you can't really have a good healthy relationship because it's boring. The thing is neither of us seems to be able to resist any temptation. I've always said that a man walks within ten feet of Alison and we're in bed. I sleep with everybody now. And I'm still considered the good girl— I'm the good slut.

What do you think Alison's favorite album is?

The Village People's *Live and Sleazy*. That was the first album I ever bought. My big sister told me that was the album to get. I was so proud of it.

What are your favorite Melrose Place *episodes?*

The most fun I had was when Alison was drunk. I had a blast being able to be strong, loud, and obnoxious because Alison always has to pull back and be sweet in the end. Those were five fun episodes.

How has Melrose Place *changed your life?*

It's been overwhelmingly positive. There's financial security, and a great place for me to come to work. The crew is amazing, the cast is great, which is rare. I also like the consistency. To be an actor and able to say, "I'm going to work today," is weird and wonderful.

What's the best thing a fan ever sent you?

I don't get sent much stuff. It seems like the boys get more stuff. The best thing that was ever sent that I saw was when Andrew got a T-shirt with a picture of him taken from *Seventeen* magazine. He wouldn't wear a T-shirt of himself, so I took that one.

When did you know that the show was a hit?

When we got bathrooms in our dressing rooms. That was the key moment for me.

Can you sum up the Melrose Place *philosophy?*

Take no responsibility and sleep with it.

"I'd have to say that my favorite Melrose Place character was always Courtney Thorne-Smith as Alison. She was clearly drawn by the writers as the good girl from the Midwest, but she in fact came off as the single scariest, meanest, most manipulative woman in all of television. I just love the way that she makes absolutely everything a huge drama. It made my skin crawl every time she'd come home and tell Billy that they "had to talk." It seemed like the writers on the show thought she was one of the more stable ones in the building, but to me she's the woman character on the show I would most want to warn my male friends to stay away from. Sydney's a much safer bet. Alison was truly frightening, and of course it was her persona I'd take on at the Melrose parties."

—Julia Sweeney, comedienne and actress (*Saturday Night Live, It's Pat, Pulp Fiction*), who had *Melrose Place* viewing parties for a year and a half. Party-goers viewed taped episodes so they could have instant replay.

Getting Neighborly: A Highly Competitive Melrose Quiz

As Amanda Woodward once said—or was it Vince Lombardi?—"Winning isn't everything. It's the only thing." With that sort of zeal for victory in mind, go ahead and try your hand at this tough but fair test of your *Melrose* wits. As far as scoring—always an important activity on *Melrose Place*—count each question in the quiz as one point. You will not be marked on a curve. Good luck, or as Amanda might put it, "Don't blow it, Alison, because when you fall this time, I won't be there to catch you."

Multiple *Melrose*

1. What were the first words spoken in the *Melrose Place* pilot?

    a. "It was the best of times. It was the worst of times."
    b. "Call me Ishmael."
    c. "It was a dark and stormy night."
    d. "Good morning, Los Angeles."

Andrew Semel

The men of *Melrose* grin and bear it.

2. Which of the following is *not* a *Beverly Hills, 90210* character who's made a guest appearance on *Melrose Place*?
a. Kelly Taylor
b. Steve Sanders
c. Lyle Menendez
d. Donna Martin

3. What film director was behind the camera for the pilot episode of *Melrose Place*?
a. Ben Stiller (*Reality Bites*)
b. Howard Deutch (*Pretty in Pink*)
c. Akira Kurosawa (*Rashomon*)
d. Quentin Tarantino (*Pulp Fiction*)

4. What role did Grant Show play on *Ryan's Hope*?
a. Ryan
b. Hope
c. Officer Rick Hyde
d. A surly rabbinical student

5. Who's never made a guest appearance on *Melrose Place*?
a. Dr. Ruth Westheimer
b. Rae Dawn Chong
c. Ann B. Davis
d. Chuck Woolery

6. Who was on the receiving end of Courtney Thorne-Smith's first on-screen kiss?
a. Andrew Shue, in *Melrose Place*
b. Rex Smith, in *Sooner or Later*
c. Charlie Sheen, in *Lucas*
d. Jason Bateman, in *Teen Wolf Too*

7. Which of the following is not a job Billy Campbell has had?
a. A junior editor at *Escapade* magazine
b. A dance teacher at Arthur Murray

    c. A department store Santa Claus

    d. A pet detective

8. What's the name of the sanitarium to which Sydney is confined?

    a. Happy Hookers

    b. Hidden Hills

    c. Happy Hours

    d. Hidden Whores

9. What's the name of the clothing designer Jane works for in the first season?

    a. Bob Mackie

    b. Donna Karan

    c. Mr. Blackwell

    d. Kay Beacon

10. What acclaimed writer does Jo turn Jake on to during the first season?

    a. William Carlos Williams

    b. F. Scott Fitzgerald

    c. Franz Kafka

    d. Howard Stern

11. What does Jo name her baby?

    a. Dallas

    b. Austin

    c. Houston

    d. El Paso

12. Which of the following is *not* the title of a television movie in which Heather Locklear has appeared?

    a. *Her Wicked Ways*

    b. *Rich Men, Single Women*

    c. *The Girl That Got Away . . . with Murder*

    d. *Highway Casanova*

13. Who owned the *Melrose* apartment complex before Amanda bought it?

a. Mr. Kaye

b. Mr. Spelling

c. Mr. Ed

d. Mister Mister

14. Which of the following messages was prominently displayed on a poster in Billy's and Alison's apartment?

a. "Poverty Sucks"

b. "So Many Men, So Little Time"

c. "Advertising Kills"

d. "You Don't Have to Be Crazy to Live Here, but It Sure Helps"

15. What's the name of the charter boat on which Reed and Jo battle to the death?

a. *The Pretty Lady*

b. *The Battered Lady*

c. *The Much-Put-Upon Lady*

d. *The Incarcerated Lady*

16. Which of the following is not a place that Matt has worked?

a. Wilshire Memorial Hospital

b. A halfway house for runaway teens

c. The Virgin Megastore

d. Bikini Burger

17. Who does Amanda tell Billy was once her role model?

a. Golda Meir

b. Peggy Fleming

c. Georgia O'Keefe

d. Ivan the Terrible

18. What's the first ad campaign that Alison and Amanda work on together?

a. Breath Assure

b. Maximum Advantage Underwear

    c. Shooter's bar
    d. The video release of *Return of Swamp Thing*

19. Which publication did Billy write for?
    a. *Guns & Ammo*
    b. *Melrose Weekly*
    c. *Modern Maturity*
    d. *Codependency Digest*

20. What's the name of the adult club where Sydney strips?
    a. The Body Stocking Club
    b. Devil's Candy Store
    c. House of Blues
    d. The Snake Pit

Melrose Matching

Match the character name with the appropriate description:

21. The peeping handy man

22. Sydney's Hollywood madam

23. D&D's most ambitious intern

24. Jo's drug-dealing love interest

25. Hillary's creepy fiancé

26. Matt's man in uniform

27. Michael's pal who wants Jane

28. Alison's high-tech hunk

29. Jane's divorce lawyer/lover

30. Jake's biological dad

a. Reed Carter

b. Steve McMillan

c. Ted Ramsey

d. Sam Towler

e. Lauren Etheridge

f. Vince Conners

g. Robert Wilson

h. Brooke Armstrong

i. Jeffrey Lindley

j. Chas Russell

True or False

31. Billy's journalistic achievements include covering a dog wedding.

32. Alison comes from Nebraska.

33. Doug Savant appears with Rob Lowe in the film *Masquerade*.

34. Vanessa Williams appears in the film *New Jack City*.

35. Josie Bissett appears in the film *Reservoir Dogs*.

36. *Melrose Place* creator Darren Star wrote the movie *If Looks Could Kill,* starring Richard Grieco.

37. Billy's father wanted him to take over the family business, Campbell's soups.

38. Alison cleans up her act at the famed Betty Ford Center.

39. Billy scored 1300 on his SATs.

40. *Melrose Place* executive producer Aaron Spelling once acted in an episode of *Gunsmoke*.

More Multiple *Melrose*

41. Which actress played Jake's mother in the "Burned" episode during the first season?
    a. Barbara Feldon
    b. Suzanne Pleshette
    c. Anita Morris
    d. Pam Grier

42. What former associate appeared to Amanda in a series of vivid, upsetting dreams?

a. Joan Collins
b. William Shatner
c. The peeping handy man
d. Her late boss Bruce

43. Which of the following is *not* a film in which Daphne Zuniga has appeared?

a. *The Sure Thing*
b. *Gross Anatomy*
c. Mel Brooks's *Spaceballs*
d. *Thelma and Louise*

44. Which of the following *Melrose* types attended Michael's and Sydney's seaside wedding?

a. Amanda and her father
b. Dr. Stanley Levin and his wife
c. Jane and Jake
d. None of the above

45. Why do new roommates Billy and Alison argue in the pilot episode?

a. He wanted to be able to have some of her peanut butter
b. He never once said to her, "I miss you"
c. She accidentally burned his novel *Taxi Confessions*
d. She blamed him for all the troubles in Bosnia

46. What television series did Josie Bissett appear in before *Melrose Place*?

a. *Alf*
b. *The Hogan Family*
c. *Double Trouble*
d. *Max Headroom*

47. Where did Billy live before moving into the *Melrose Place* complex?

a. In Beverly Hills with the Walsh family
b. In Brentwood with the Simpsons
c. In the San Fernando Valley with his parents
d. In Zimbabwe with his soccer team

48. What role did Courtney Thorne-Smith play in her Montessori preschool production of *Snow White and the Seven Dwarfs*?

a. Dopey
b. Sneezy
c. Whiny, the advertising dwarf
d. Grumpy

49. Which composer wrote the *Melrose Place* theme music?

a. Tim Truman
b. Bess Truman
c. Tim Burton
d. Courtney Love

50. Which of the following significant events or issues have *not* been dealt with on *Melrose Place*?

a. The L.A. riots
b. AIDS
c. Gays in the military
d. The bankruptcy of Orange County

More *Melrose* Matching

51. Susan Madsen   a. Alison's record industry party boy
52. Terrence Haggardy   b. Jake's damsel in distress
53. Zack Phillips   c. Alison's friendly tennis star

54. Sara   d. Rhonda's wealthy fiancé

55. Rex Weldon   e. Abused future *Models inc.* beauty

56. Brittany   f. Billy's tasty Cordon Bleu chef

The Real Thing

Identify which of the following lines of dialogue are genuine *Melrose Place* dialogue and which are cheap fakes.

57. "What in God's name is Matt doing with the mailman?"
—Amanda

58. "Okay, guys, who peed in the swimming pool?" —Jake

59. "Alison, I want you to be my partner for life . . . forever."
—Billy

60. "He's very good at what he does—sometimes too good for his own good" —Amanda

61. "Mancini, I don't care if you're starving, get your stinking hands off that cadaver!" —Dr. Stanley Levin.

62. "So tell me, Sydney, exactly what was it that made you want to become a soldier of fortune?" —A paramilitary recruiting office representative

63. "I'm not going to be your boy toy, Amanda! Either share some of your self with me or you cut me loose." —Jake

64. "Did you see that little tramp's face? I thought she was going to throw up when you walked in there." —Michael

65. "Hey, does anybody here know what the hell happened to Sandy's southern accent?" —Matt

66. "I'm living in a building of voyeurs!" —Sandy

67. "Broken ribs . . . hmm, I'm surprised. I told them to break your arm." —Kimberly

68. "My big surprise—I'm buying the building!" —Amanda

69. "Michael, don't you get horny anymore?" —Jane

70. "Sorry, Kimberly, no pitchforks allowed on the beach." —Michael

Q & A

71. What's the name of the hospital where Michael, Kimberly, and Matt have worked?

72. Which character did Doug Savant play on the series *Knot's Landing*?

73. What's the name of the youth service organization cofounded by Andrew Shue?

74. What's Alison's nickname for her beloved old car in the first season?

75. Which disease did Michael diagnose Amanda as having?

More True or False

76. Since she's left, Matt's never mentioned his pal Rhonda.

77. Amanda's first word on the show was "bitch."

78. Alison's bra size —as of the first season—was 34D.

79. Someone has skinny dipped in the *Melrose Place* pool.

80. Actress Deborah Adair—who played Amanda and Alison's D&D boss Lucy—is in real life married to *Melrose Place* producer Chip Hayes.

81. *Melrose* guest star Traci Lords's early career included memorable appearances in numerous religious films.

82. *Melrose Place* was awarded a 1993 Media Award for outstanding dramatic television series by GLADD (Gay and Lesbian Alliance Against Defamation).

83. Syd has had a poster of the Carpenters tribute album on display in her apartment.

84. Josie Bissett plays the wife of guitarist Robbie Krieger in the film *The Doors*.

Even More *Melrose* Matching

85. Brooke's sugar daddy
86. Amanda's doctor boyfriend
87. Jo's nanny from hell
88. D&D efficiency expert
89. Alison's football sex maniac

a. Katlin Mills
b. Hayley Armstrong
c. Terry Parsons
d. Emily Baldwin
e. Peter Burns

Even More Multiple *Melrose*

90. Where did Chris Marchette ultimately take Sydney when he kidnapped her?
a. An abandoned wheat silo
b. A rowdy Australian pub
c. A dangerous South Central flophouse
d. A swanky Las Vegas hotel suite

91. How does Jake react when Billy asks him to be his best man at his wedding to Alison?
a. He embraces Billy
b. He punches Billy
c. He embraces Matt
d. He harpoons Billy

92. At what school did Billy attend college?
a. The Hollywood School of Journalism
b. Dartmouth College
c. Cornell University
d. Southern Methodist University

93. Which of the following publications has *never* had a photograph of a *Melrose Place* cast member grace its cover?
a. *Soap Opera Hairstyles*
b. *Diet & Exercise*
c. *The New Yorker*
d. *The National Enquirer*

94. Which of the following is *not* a job that Jake's had on *Melrose Place*?
a. Espresso café worker
b. Construction worker
c. Motorcycle mechanic
d. Hostage negotiator

95. Which of the following recording artists does *not* appear on the *Melrose Place—The Music* soundtrack album?

a. Paul Westerberg
b. Annie Lennox
c. Jack Wagner
d. Sam Phillips

96. Courtney Thorne-Smith appeared in *Revenge of the Nerds II*. What was the subtitle of that epic?

a. *A Long Day's Journey into Nerds*
b. *Adventures in the Ad Game*
c. *Nerds in Paradise*
d. *Nerds on Melrose*

97. How old was Darren Star when he wrote the pilot of *Melrose Place*'s mothership, *Beverly Hills, 90210*?

a. Twenty-eight
b. Sixteen
c. Thirty-four
d. Fifty-eight

98. What does Alison's sister, Meredith, do for a living?

a. She's a family counselor
b. She's a stand-up comedian
c. She's a librarian
d. She manages a grunge band from Seattle

99. For what professional sports team did Andrew Shue play?

a. The Los Angeles Dodgers baseball team
b. The Philadelphia Freedom tennis team
c. The Burbank Bruisers bowling team
d. The Bulawyo Highlanders soccer team

100. What's the name of Jo's abusive ex-husband?

a. Charles Reynolds
b. Rich Reynolds
c. Burt Reynolds
d. Orenthal James Reynolds

Scoring Guide

100 points:

Congratulations, you've scored like Michael Mancini at the Andrews family picnic. Please consider yourself an honorary member of the show's extended cast. We'll see you for celebratory drinks at Shooters!

99–81 points:

You're a legitimate—or for our purposes should that really be illegitimate?—*Melrose* expert. Good job, you're on Amanda's waiting list for the next available apartment in the complex.

80–51 points:

Well, at least you're in the neighborhood. And don't worry because it happens to be a very lovely neighborhood.

50–31 points:

Gosh, you really must know a tremendous amount about *Home Improvement*.

30–0 points:

Frankly, you're in trouble. You probably think Jake is a Hemingway character.

Answers

1. d, 2. c, 3. b, 4. c, 5. c, 6. a, 7. d, 8. b, 9. d, 10. a,
11. b, 12. c, 13. a, 14. c, 15. a, 16. c, 17. c, 18. b, 19. b, 20. a
21. c, 22. e, 23. h, 24. a, 25. j, 26. i, 27. d, 28. b, 29. g, 30. f
31. True
32. False, she's from Wisconsin
33. True
34. True
35. False
36. True
37. False, the family business is Campbell & Sons furniture store
38. False, she rehabs at Twin Oaks
39. True
40. True
41. c, 42. d, 43. d, 44. d, 45. a, 46. b, 47. c, 48. a, 49. a, 50. d
51. f, 52. d, 53. a, 54. e, 55. c, 56. b
57. Fake
58. Fake
59. Real
60. Real
61. Fake
62. Fake
63. Real
64. Real
65. Fake
66. Real
67. Real
68. Real
69. Real
70. Fake
71. Wilshire Memorial Hospital
72. The young Mack McKenzie
73. Do Something!
74. Betsy
75. Hodgkin's disease
76. False
77. False

78. True
79. True, Alison and Zack Phillips
80. True
81. False
82. True
83. True
84. True
85. b, 86. e, 87. d, 88. a, 89. c
90. d, 91. b, 92. d, 93. c, 94. d, 95. c,
96. c, 97. a, 98. c, 99. d, 100. a

A Melrosian Recipe Revealed!

Okay, maybe you're thinking *The Official Melrose Place Companion* is kind of a fluffy read. Sure, it's fun, but what practical purpose does this book serve? In a superficial effort to be more substantial, we present you with the original recipe for the wedding cake of first-season characters Rhonda and Terrence. Award-winning pastry chef and restaurateur Nancy Silverton of L.A.'s Campanile prepared the cake and even made a cameo appearance on *Melrose* along with her tasty creation. Here—courtesy of Silverton—are the complete directions that will allow you to share some of Rhonda and Terrence's bliss by having your cake and eating it too.

Free of *Melrose*, Rhonda and Terrence are almost guaranteed a happy marriage.

Doug Hyun

Nancy's Easy Fancy Wedding Cake

Devil's Food Cake

2 tablespoons butter, melted
6 tablespoons unsweetened cocoa powder
2½ ounces bittersweet chocolate
3 tablespoons water
8 tablespoons (1 stick) unsalted butter at room temperature
¾ cup dark brown sugar, gently packed
4 eggs, separated
¼ cup sour cream
1¼ teaspoons baking soda
1 teaspoon boiling water (to infuse baking soda)
1¼ cups all-purpose flour, sifted
2 tablespoons granulated sugar
White Mountain Frosting (recipe follows)

Brush an 8-inch round cake pan with some of the melted butter. Line the bottom of the pan with a round of parchment paper. Brush with butter again. Chill briefly to solidify butter. Dust with 2 tablespoons of the cocoa powder, and knock out excess. Set aside.

Preheat oven to 350°F. Adjust oven rack to the middle position.

Cut the chocolate into 2-inch pieces. In a heatproof bowl, melt the chocolate over barely simmering water. (The water should not touch the bottom of the bowl or the chocolate will burn.) Turn off heat and let stand over warm water until ready to use.

In a small saucepan, whisk together the 3 tablespoons of water and the remaining cocoa powder. Bring to a simmer over medium heat, whisking constantly, until the mixture is smooth and thickened and the whisk leaves an empty trail when it is drawn across the bottom of the pan. Remove from heat. Whisk in the melted chocolate. Set aside in a warm place.

Using the paddle attachment of an electric mixer, beat the butter on medium speed until it whitens and holds soft peaks, 3 to 5 minutes. Beat in the brown sugar and combine well. Turn the mixer to low and add the egg yolks one at a time, scraping down the sides of the bowl as necessary. Stir in the chocolate mixture and sour cream.

Dissolve the baking soda in the boiling water, making sure that the baking soda fizzes. Beat half the flour into the batter, add the baking soda, then beat in the remaining flour. Set aside.

Using the whisk attachment of an electric mixer, beat the egg whites on low speed until frothy. Turn the mixer to medium and beat until soft peaks form. Turn the mixer to high and gradually beat in the granulated sugar until stiff, glossy peaks form.

Whisk one-third of the egg whites into the batter to lighten, then fold in the rest of the egg whites, incorporating well. Pour the batter into the cake pan. Bake for 25 minutes, until the cake shrinks slightly from the sides of the pan and is slightly soft in the center.

When thoroughly cool, remove the cake from the pan. With a serrated knife, trim the rounded top of the cake so it is flat, and cut the cake horizontally into thirds so that the layers are no thicker than ½ inch. Place one cake layer on a serving platter or cardboard round, trimmed side up, and spread the top with ⅛ inch of frosting. Place the second layer on top, press down lightly, and spread it with frosting. Top with the third cake layer and press down lightly. Spread frosting on the sides of cake. Chill to firm.

Hold the cake flat on your palm for easy handling. Plop the remaining frosting on the top of the cake and spread it with a back and forth motion, using a long-bladed spatula held flat against the top of the cake. Allow the frosting to flow over the edges of the top. When the top is smooth, use the spatula to spread the frosting down the sides of the cake in broad, smooth strokes, turning the cake after each stroke.

Cut the cake into 8 to 10 pieces and serve.

White Mountain Frosting

2 cups sugar
¾ cup water
3 tablespoons light corn syrup
4 egg whites
2 tablespoons vanilla extract
½ teaspoon almond extract

In a medium-size saucepan, combine the sugar, water, and corn syrup, and stir over low heat until the sugar is dissolved. Bring to a boil. When the syrup boils it will throw sugar onto the sides of the pan. At that point, wash down the sides of the pan with a pastry brush, dipping the pastry brush in water as necessary. Boil gently for 5 minutes or until the syrup reaches 270°F. Remove from heat and set aside.

Using an electric mixer on low speed, beat the egg whites until soft peaks are formed. Then, slowly, in a steady stream, pour the sugar syrup into the egg whites until all the sugar syrup is incorporated. Continue beating mixture for 2 to 3 minutes. Gently fold in the vanilla and almond extracts with the fewest number of strokes. Use frosting immediately.

Thomas Calabro:
Q & A

A wonderfully reprehen-
sible villain in a series with no
shortage of such characters, *Melrose
Place*'s own satanic love machine, Dr.
Michael Mancini, is truly the sort of
guy everyone loves to hate. Over the
course of three seasons, Michael has
gone through a truly remarkable
transformation—a devolution,
you might even say. When we
all first met the Mancinis,
Michael and Jane were
young newlyweds trying to
find time for one another
in their new lives in Los
Angeles. Michael was
serving double-duty as an
ambitious intern at
Wilshire Memorial Hospital
and, lest we forget, as *Melrose Place*'s apartment man-
ager. Apparently, the strain
of these responsibilities took
its toll on the guy. Since then,
the not-so-good doctor has
been making up for lost time,

Andrew Semel

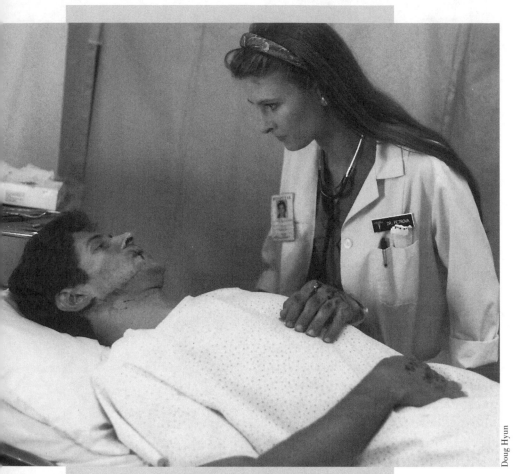

From Russia with love: Katya displays glasnost as she comforts an ailing Michael at Wilshire Memorial.

even making time with Jane's little sister, Sydney. Along the way, this oddly seductive hypocrite has broken more than just the Hippocratic oath. Brooklyn-born Thomas Calabro has embraced Michael's turn to the dark side with tremendous zest and style. Ironically, Calabro got his start in a grade-school production of *Jesus Christ Superstar.* A gifted New York theater actor who went on to star in the short-lived TV series *Dream Street,* Calabro has now truly earned his doctorate for playing bad and making it feel so good.

What impact would you say Melrose Place *has had on your life?*

I'm paying a mortgage instead of rent. Any medium can be powerful. It's a money thing when you come down to it. And now I can afford to do what I want to do.

What do fans ask you when they write you?

They ask me for my phone number usually.

Do you watch the show?

Of course, it's part of my job.

When do you think Michael went bad?

He never went bad. He just kinda went. He just does what he does out of a sense of preservation.

Wayne Stambler

What kind of reaction did you get from fans on the street when your character started to turn toward the dark side?

Men would say, "Stay away from my wife." Women would ask me, "How can you do what you're doing to Jane?" But people were still attracted to the guy. I found it kind of bizarre but there you go.

Do you ever miss all the bonding of the first season?

Originally, we were the staid couple who every-

Back to back bitches: two of the misunderstood women in Michael's life.

one else in the building came to for advice. There wasn't drama in that. Fortunately, then they saw what happened between Marcia and me—I should say between Kimberly and Michael—and they really ran with that.

Does Melrose Place *have a moral message—like, say, go ahead and sleep with your wife's sister?*

No, we say don't. We're the outlet so you don't have to do it. We save you the trouble. I certainly hope nobody goes around doing the things we do.

Timothy White

Behind the scenes, would you say things are competitive in the cast?

No, people have asked me about that. They wanted to know if I ever wanted more close-ups. Come on, we all know what we're doing here. No one's counting scenes.

How does doing Melrose *compare to doing theater?*

Melrose Place is not like being in a play like *Orphans* or something. That's obvious, but that doesn't mean I can't do my job and do it well.

"Melrose Place *is just so fabulous. I haven't missed one episode in two seasons. Not one. That first show was so juicy that I just said, 'God that was good.' After that, I found myself on Monday nights in the recording studio thinking, 'Okay, it's* Melrose *time, maybe I'll finish singing this song in an hour.' Even when I'm in London, I have tapes Federal Expressed.*

"To me Melrose Place *is the classic struggle between good and evil. There's nothing like a good story line with some real drama. I love all the cliffhangers and the bigger-than-life quality of the show. You've also got to consider that sex sells and* Melrose *proves that—there's nobody ugly on the show! In terms of favorite characters, you've got to love Amanda, Sydney, and Michael. God, I think Michael's one of the coolest guys—the way he casts his fate to the wind kills me. And even though it doesn't reflect any of my own behavior, I've got to admit that I love all the bed-hopping on the show. I love it."*

—Luther Vandross, soul singer and major *Melrose* lover

Josie Bissett: Q & A

In those good old *Melrose* days of yore, it seemed like Jane Mancini's biggest problem was getting her inattentive physician husband to play doctor with her a little more often. Jane must be one of the most attractive sexually frustrated women in all of pop culture history. Things have only gotten worse since then. Truth be told, Jane has subsequently had an especially horrible run of bad luck. Her marriage was destroyed by her husband's flagrant infidelity, while her relationship with her little sister was wrecked by . . . well, by her little sister, really. Meanwhile, Jane's love life has mostly been a series of traumatic misfires and her promising fashion career has been a roller-coaster. However, if Jane's suffered at the hands of various creeps—and, boy, has Jane suffered at the hands of various creeps—she certainly has suffered exquisitely. Playing Jane's pain beautifully is the decidedly ungrungy Seattle native Josie Bissett, whose every haircut has been closely studied by many *Melrose* fashion mavens around the world. A model from the age of twelve, Bissett went on to appear on various series, including *The Hogan Family* and *Doogie Howser, M.D.* At one acting audition, she met her future husband, Rob Estes, who's familiar as the star of the series *Silk Stalkings.* Sweetly, Estes also appeared as *Melrose Place*'s own Sam Towler, the old friend of Michael's who always carried a torch for Jane. And why wouldn't he?

Diego Uchitel

Can you offer any theories on why none of the characters on the show seem to use the pool much anymore?

All the blond hairs turned green.

And why's the laundry room been seen so rarely?

It got destroyed in the earthquake.

Do you ever miss all the bonding and good will among the cast members from the first season of the show?

No. The bonding we did was unrealistic.

What three words do you think best describe Jane?

Forgiving, loyal, and doormat.

What's your favorite episode of Melrose Place*?*

The one when Jane has a one-night stand with Michael, then dogs him.

What couple that hasn't happened yet on the show would you most like to see happen?

Matt and Jake.

How would you say that the show has changed over the seasons?

It's gone from realism to bed-hopping, baby-stealing, cult-following, killing, etc.

Who would you most like to see move into the Melrose Place *complex?*

Forrest Gump.

What's the biggest difference between you and Jane?

I'm not a victim.

Wayne Stambler

The Andrews sisters: sibling rivalry was never more stunning.

Happier Days: The Mancinis before the fall.

Timothy White

Who's the most surprising Melrose Place fan that you've encountered?

An eighty-year-old woman I met.

Which departed character would you most like to see return to the show?

Rhonda.

Does life ever imitate Melrose Place?

No way, or at least very rarely.

What's your favorite line of dialogue you've spoken on the show?

Jane says to Michael after a one-night stand: "You were great, babe!"

How about a least favorite?

"Oh my God."

How has Melrose Place changed your life?

It's given me lots of other business opportunities.

And how would you sum up the Melrose Place philosophy, such as it is?

Sleep with thy neighbor.

Laura Leighton: Q & A

Sydney Andrews has been a brave and adorable pioneer in the field of sibling rivalry. If it's taboo, Syd can, in all good conscience—or should that be all bad conscience—say "been there, done that, on at least one episode." Originally envisioned as just an annoying temporary guest at 4616 Melrose Place, Sydney became one of those characters that's simply so winning that the show had to find more room at the inn for her. A large part of the reason for Syd's remarkable staying power is the ironic all-American-girl-gone-wrong charm that Laura Leighton brings to the role. Amazingly, this lovely, wholesome-looking Iowa native made her professional acting debut on *Melrose Place* in 1992. Leighton did, however, tour nationally as a singer and dancer with a rather squeaky-clean troupe called the Young Americans—about as un-Sydney-like a gig as one could imagine.

Who are the most surprising Melrose Place *fans you've met?*

I guess what surprises me the most are all the six- and seven-year-olds. Maybe I should say that their parents surprise me by letting them watch the show. They ask me for my autograph, and I have to ask, "How old are you anyway?"

Do the kiddies have lots of questions about prostitution?

It blows my mind that they watch.

Diego Uchitel

Why? Are you worried that perhaps Syd's not the best role model?

I tell them, *Please*, don't watch this show.

So how come nobody uses the pool much lately?

There have been some mysterious items floating in the pool at times, and I think that the characters have boycotted it ever since then.

So you personally don't use the pool in your free time?

No, but the pool has been used as punishment for various people in the cast and crew.

Do you think anyone in the cast misses all the bonding and good will of the first season?

Well, I haven't heard anyone longing for those days when Billy not being able to get a credit card would be an entire episode. Or when the washing machine being broken was a big deal. I haven't heard any "remember whens."

How much rent do you think Syd pays?

I believe that it's seven hundred fifty. That would be a real bargain, though there's some confusion about whether she has a studio or a one-bedroom.

Is that difficult motivationally for you as an actress?

It keeps me up at night.

I feel you play her as a person with a studio, with the accompanying sense of claustrophobia.

See, you've been paying attention. But my favorite scene—which never made it to the show—is when Sydney finds her bedroom. All this time she thinks she has a studio, then when it comes time for her to get a roommate for a few episodes, she discovers she's accidentally been sleeping in her living room.

Are you aware that one of the only contradictions in the whole series is that in one of the first episodes Jane says she's an only child?

Why do you think Sydney is so messed up? Jane has absolutely denied her from the start! That's the problem.

What couple that you haven't seen on the show would you like to see most?

Amanda and Alison.

Diego Uchitel

Sydney and Michael: They make a lovely young couple.

How have things changed behind the scenes at Melrose?

I wasn't here from day one, but I know the atmosphere has always been really easygoing. Everyone meshed. It's always been a very meshable group.

What's the attraction of Michael for all these women? Do you imagine he's fantastic in bed?

I wouldn't say he's fantastic in bed. I don't think even Sydney thinks that! I think the attraction is that she wants to be the one to tame him.

Do you think Billy and Alison should get married?

No, they shouldn't get married. In the real world, two people with that many problems should never get married.

Have you ever gone to a Melrose-*viewing party?*

I've never attended one of the rumored fanatic parties that I hear about. I watch with a small group of close friends with whom I can watch with one or maybe two eyes covered.

What's Syd's favorite album?

Hmm . . . I guess she's a Seattle grunge kind of gal.

What's a memorable episode for Sydney?

The entire Sydney and Michael wedding was pretty memorable. I definitely remember swimming in that wedding dress. We had one take to get that scene. Otherwise we had to take all that time to dry off everything again. I remember being pulled out of the water and realizing I still had my pumps on and my veil, too.

What do you think the appeal of the show is?

It's cheap thrills with a twisted sense of reality. I think people enjoy watching a worst-case scenario. I think that's why it's fun.

What's the question that Melrose *fans ask you the most?*

"Is that your real hair color?"

And?

You think I'm going to tell you *that?*

Marcia Cross:
Q & A

Kimberly Shaw—that's Dr. Kimberly Shaw to you, buster—proves conclusively that the Other Woman is not always merely a passing fancy. Appearing late in the first season of *Melrose Place* as the extracurricular love interest of Michael Mancini, this intense couple was soon infusing Wilshire Memorial Hospital's medical environment with nearly lethal levels of sexual heat. Not even death—or some reasonable facsimile thereof—could keep Kimberly away. Even after her famous near-death experience, Kim returned to kill Michael, then stuck around to love him. Perhaps that helps explain why all these seasons, she's still very much in the picture. Marcia Cross's background has made her perfectly prepared for the rigorous demands of being Kimberly. After studying drama at the Juilliard School, Cross did soap operas and other TV shows, appeared in the film *Bad Influence,* and acted in a number of Shakespearean plays at various prestigious theaters. During the 1994 summer hiatus, for instance, Cross played Viola in *Twelfth Night* at the Old Globe Theatre in San Diego. As for Dr. Shaw, Cross advises us that the current diagnosis is that she's here to stay.

Medically speaking, is it safe to say Kim's pretty whacked out?

She's whacked. Completely.

Has your Shakespearean training prepared you for Melrose?

I always think in my head that Tom and I are like Macbeth and Lady

Macbeth. What's the difference? Of course, it's different, but it's really not in some ways. Greek tragedy. Shakespeare. They're all full of huge, emotional plots. Who knows, maybe watching *Hamlet* or *Macbeth* was like watching the soap opera of the time.

What was your favorite episode?

Probably the most important for me was the first one. Initially, I was only hired for one episode. But I think there was just some kind of spark that was there between Tom and me. Something happened at the end of our scene in front of the vending machine at the hospital—a moment of chemistry between Kimberly and Michael that was cut back a little in the editing because it got a little too much, too hot. Risking complete narcissism, I would have to say my own favorite episode was my return from the so-called dead. I loved the ambiguity of the scenes and the danger between Kimberly and Michael. Toying with him was absolutely delicious.

Speaking of Michael, is it your reading of the material that part of his amazing appeal to the women of Melrose Place *is that he's great in bed?*

I don't consciously play that. I guess Kimberly and Michael walk that fine line between love and hate. If you've seen their relationship, there's no sweet, lovey dovey stuff between them. It's not about sweetness. It's about the extremes.

Do you think anyone in the cast misses all the goodwill and the bonding of the first season?

Are you holding me responsible?

Partly. After all, you certainly helped turn Michael to the dark side.

Oh yeah, I'm definitely responsible for that.

What do Melrose Place *fans say to you when they spot you?*

People are great when they see me. They look at me and they get this crazy look in their eyes. I thought in the beginning they were going to hate me. And when that whole baby-stealing plot came up I thought that was it. I am out of here. And instead people just get this glint in their eyes and tell me, "Oh, we love your character." So that makes me very happy.

What do you think Kimberly's favorite album is?

I don't know. Some Beethoven. Or Tchaikovsky. Actually, I think it's Sibelius—something very melodramatic. Maybe Violin Concerto no. 1. It starts off with this really painful violin solo, and that's kind of where she's coming from.

Any theories why nobody on the show uses the pool much anymore?

Couldn't say. Kimberly's never been in the pool.

How about you?

I personally have never been in the pool, and you don't need to tell anybody that because then I might wind up in there one day. They'll make sure I get a dunking.

What three adjectives would you say best describe Kimberly?

Sweet, misunderstood, and vulnerable—go figure.

Kimberly decides a massive overdose will solve all her problems. It didn't.

Doug Hyun

So do you think Kimberly will ever end up living at 4616 Melrose Place?

I don't know if they'd ever welcome me in the building. My mother said, "How could you live in that apartment building with all those people?" Guess she didn't like the idea.

Melrose Place®: A User's Guide

Billy
Dated Amanda; got her pregnant; tried marrying Alison; dated Brooke and married her instead.

Amanda
Took over D&D; bought 4616 Melrose; diagnosed with non-Hodgkin's lymphoma; took leave of D&D; proposed to by Michael; turned him down; recovered and returned to D&D, firing Alison.

Brooke
World's most ambitious advertising intern spied on Alison for Amanda while Amanda was in the hospital; shipped Alison off to work in Hong Kong while she worked on Billy.

Hillary
Amanda's dear old mom who abandoned her; forced Amanda to do business with her company, Models inc.; her fiancé hit on Amanda.

Jo
Lived with Jake; met Reed at high school reunion; after he got her pregnant, she harpooned and shot him; dated Jess.

Alison
Rose from humble receptionist to assistant account executive to president of D&D; lived with Billy; almost married Billy, but sidetracked by abusive dad; on-off-on-again relationship with Billy since; developed drinking problem; recovered; now jobless and Billy-less.

Jess
Put hit on brother Jake; proposed to Jo; when she declined, he beat her.

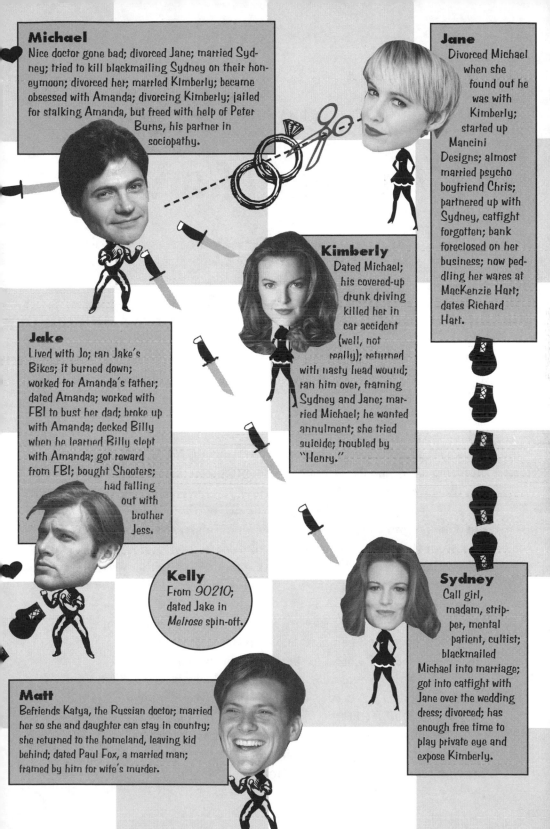

Michael
Nice doctor gone bad; divorced Jane; married Sydney; tried to kill blackmailing Sydney on their honeymoon; divorced her; married Kimberly; became obsessed with Amanda; divorcing Kimberly; jailed for stalking Amanda, but freed with help of Peter Burns, his partner in sociopathy.

Jane
Divorced Michael when she found out he was with Kimberly; started up Mancini Designs; almost married psycho boyfriend Chris; partnered up with Sydney, catfight forgotten; bank foreclosed on her business; now peddling her wares at MacKenzie Hart; dates Richard Hart.

Kimberly
Dated Michael; his covered-up drunk driving killed her in car accident (well, not really); returned with nasty head wound; ran him over, framing Sydney and Jane; married Michael; he wanted annulment; she tried suicide; troubled by "Henry."

Jake
Lived with Jo; ran Jake's Bikes; it burned down; worked for Amanda's father; dated Amanda; worked with FBI to bust her dad; broke up with Amanda; decked Billy when he learned Billy slept with Amanda; got reward from FBI; bought Shooters; had falling out with brother Jess.

Kelly
From 90210; dated Jake in Melrose spin-off.

Matt
Befriends Katya, the Russian doctor; married her so she and daughter can stay in country; she returned to the homeland, leaving kid behind; dated Paul Fox, a married man; framed by him for wife's murder.

Sydney
Call girl, madam, stripper, mental patient, cultist; blackmailed Michael into marriage; got into catfight with Jane over the wedding dress; divorced; has enough free time to play private eye and expose Kimberly.

A Sense of Place: Memories of a Visit to the Melrose Set

I t's less a trip, really, than a pilgrimage.

Even after a number of visits, there's something spiritually uplifting about the experience of going to the *Melrose Place* set. To get there one must travel a considerable distance from Hollywood, past the epicenter of the famed Northridge earthquake, which once gave the *Melrose* stages a savage shaking. Finally though, one reaches a veritable oasis of pop culture production.

At times, *Melrose Place* shares this facility with other productions. This morning, in fact, there's a very professional-looking elephant and a vintage airplane in the parking lot shooting scenes for *Dumbo*. Last season, things were slightly disrupted when Arnold Schwarzenegger and company invaded the area to shoot some of *True Lies*. Generally, though, there's no shortage of calm here.

Once inside, one naturally seeks to find out the answers to all sorts of nagging questions. Yes, Virginia, there *is* a pool here, and a rather beautiful one at that. Sadly, it's only heated when someone has a swimming scene—something that seems to happen less and less these days. Today, there's only one chaise lounge poolside, and no one around can determine definitively if this is the same piece of pool furniture that the now-departed character Sandy occupied with

oug Hyun

The *Melrose* courtyard is deceptively serene when the gang's away.

such zealous dedication during her brief first-season residency. The tastefully painted backdrop of the Hollywood Hills, damaged during the earthquake, is now back in its rightful place above the courtyard.

The 4616 Melrose Place laundry room—rarely seen on-screen since the first season during which it served as prime *Melrose* gathering spot—is nowhere to be seen today. "I know," says Darren Star, when queried about this disturbing and frankly unsanitary turn of events. "Every time I've wanted to put in a laundry room scene, Chip Hayes tells me what a tough set it is to put up. Fortunately, I was able to give the place a prominent appearance at the end of the third season."

Just off the pool is the most commonly seen of the *Melrose* apartments: number 3, fondly recalled as Alison's and Billy's troubled love nest. Currently, it's simply Alison's pad. At the risk of seeming nosy, I take a closer look at the assorted furnishings and personal effects here. Most fascinating are Alison's bookshelves—an archaeologically significant treasure trove for the inquiring *Melrose* mind. "The cast stole all the good books during the first season," Courtney Thorne-Smith has said. Yet, still there on the shelves are works that seem highly *Melrose*-meaningful, including *Abnormal Psychology and Modern Life, The Official Preppy Handbook, A Man and His Art* (by Frank Sinatra), *The Paris Review, Jealousy* (by Nancy Friday), *The Doctor's Wife* (a loaner from Jane?), *Lonesome Cities* (by Rod McKuen; probably something Billy left behind), and the *Rolling Stone Encyclopedia of Rock & Roll.*

Alison's kitchen. Neat and clean, it's the perfect place for a happy meal or a hellacious fight.

Doug Hyun

Wandering through the same kitchen where Alison and Billy shared so many happy and even more unhappy moments yields additional insights. The Life cereal is probably Alison's, while the more childlike Lucky Charms must have been abandoned by Billy, who's now taken up residence upstairs in number 8. Clearly, Alison's been working hard lately, since the only thing in the refrigerator is some vintage pasta. Unfortunately—and potentially uncomfortably—Alison's bathroom doesn't exist today, having been converted temporarily for filming purposes into Jo's combination bathroom and darkroom. One can tell it's Jo's because the room's been painted black.

Upon close inspection, most of the other *Melrose* apartment units turn out, disillusioningly, to be mere shells of their televised selves. Still, one can still get the lay of the land at 4616 Melrose Place. Next to Alison's, a little closer to the commonly seen mailbox area, is number 2, Matt's place. Just across the courtyard is number 5, Jane's place, and number 1, Jake's pad. The "Go Away" unwelcome mat outside of Jake's apartment suggests it's best not even to knock there. Directly upstairs from Jake in number 6 is Jo. Seeing this cozy arrangement up close evokes memories of the provocative dialogue the two shared in "House of God," Jo's first episode on the show. "You've got the best unit in the building," Jake told her meaningfully. "So I've been told," Jo responded with confident sensuality. "Your apartment," Jake explained with typical economy and strength, "it's just above mine."

Next door to Jo upstairs is where Sydney dwells, number 7, which was briefly shared in the third season with creepy, cultish roommate Rikki (Traci Lords). Next to Syd in number 8 is Billy, who still lives within Alison's sight line—this clari-fies how she hap-

Judging from his unwelcome mat, Jake enjoys his privacy.

Doug Hyun

pened to spy him cavorting with her ex-friend Susan. Conveniently close to Billy is former flame and lovely landlady, Amanda, who lives in number 4, a choice spot just off the building's dramatic east stairwell.

Outside the stage—just in front of some of the cast members Star Waggon dressing trailers—there's a *Melrose* nursery where workers care for all the flora that dots the sets. In a pinch, this area can also be turned into a garden restaurant for a romantic dining exterior scene. This is also where you'll find the commonly visited makeup and costume trailers. Farther back, there's the *Melrose* mill, which has served both as the office of Jane Mancini Designs and as the interior for the now-defunct boat *Pretty Lady*.

On the other side of the stage is the bullpen where some staff meetings take place as well as where Billy all too briefly labored for *Escapade* magazine. Also on this side of the complex is *Melrose*'s main production office—the belly of the beast. From this vantage, producer Chip Hayes mans *Melrose*'s mission control. Here the cast members pick up scripts and schedules, and production types bond freely. The office bulletin board is disarmingly wholesome with all sorts of *Melrose*-related clippings on display. Today there's a birth announcement about the new addition to the extended *Melrose* family and a notice about an upcoming softball game versus *90210*. In terms of controversy, there's one article posted regarding the banning of the show by the government of Singapore and an ad for a penile enlargement service. And lest the folks at *Melrose* forget their roots, an oversize Gap ad with a portrait of the original first-season cast still hangs proudly in a place of honor.

On a hunch that there's work to be done, I decide to check out the interior of the D&D Advertising office. Above the front entrance, a wall of clocks tells the time in a variety of cities beginning with the letter *D*—Dublin, Dresden, Denver, Dallas, and Detroit, with D&D time in the middle. At the receptionist desk, below where Alison once toiled ambitiously before her rise up the corporate ladder, there are a couple of old "while you were out" message slips left— one surmises—by some Elvis Costello–loving colleague. "To Alison," it reads, "You Know This World Is Killing You." Immediately, my mind races back to the second-season episode "The Two Mrs. Mancinis" in which Alison returns to her hometown where an old boyfriend performs a dreadful version of "My Aim Is True," the classic Costello song containing those same lyrics. Equally intriguing is another leftover message to Alison's old boss, Lucy, asking her to call home immediately. Could this be a *Melrose* in-joke, considering

that Deborah Adair—who played Lucy—is in real life married to *Melrose Place*'s Chip Hayes? More clear-cut is the fact that there's a book titled *Loving an Alcoholic* at Billy's old cubicle.

Jake's popular *Melrose* watering hole, Shooters.

Thirsty after all this strenuous investigative reporting, I stop to lift my spirits at the Shooters set. Alas, it turns out that all the liquor bottles behind the bar are dry. Except for a few wayward extras, there's not much company and good cheer to be had at Shooter's today. As if that weren't bad enough, the bar's pinball machine appears to be permanently tilt. Fortunately, the impressive jukebox

Doug Hyun

Amanda's hip apartment . . .
with books to feed a lively,
vindictive mind . . . and a
fridge stocked for the perfect
body.

Doug Hyun

Doug Hyun

offers such surefire barroom crowd-pleasers as "It Never Rains in Southern California," "I Think I Love You," "You Don't Have to Be a Star (to Be in My Show)," and "Disco Duck (Parts 1 and 2)."

Finally, it's time to get to the rather groovy interior of Amanda's pad. As it turns out, Amanda's reading selection is also wildly illuminating. A copy of Robert Schuller's *Life's Not Fair But God Is Good* clues one into Mandy's well-hidden spiritual side, while copies of *The Comedies of Shakespeare* and *Love in the Time of Cholera* indicate wide-ranging literary tastes. A book called *When Doctors Get Sick* could be borrowed from Jane. Amanda's also a bit of an aging alternative rocker with Lloyd Cole and Straightjacket Fits prominent in her CD rack. The bitchy one's refrigerator, meanwhile, is the best stocked of all the Melrose units with white wine, a Wolfgang Puck pizza, Diet Pepsi, and—most incongruous—a bottle of Manischewitz borscht with beef.

Nearby is the interior of Jane's cozy apartment, featuring that familiar cherubs print above the faux bricked-in fireplace. Her library seems revelatory as well. Who besides our Jane would have Dickens's *A Tale of Two Cities* next to *Elvis: What Happened?* Conspicuous on a table in the living room is a book titled *Readings in Developmental Psychology*, apparently reflecting Jane's moving desire on her part to better understand all of the dysfunctional people in her life.

Talking about dysfunction, neither Dr. Mancini nor Dr. Shaw are on duty at the Wilshire Memorial Hospital set at the moment. Surprisingly, the vending machine in the doctors' on-call lounge offers all sorts of unhealthy fare like Have-A-Tampa cigars and Lemonheads candy. In one of the doctor's lockers—I'm guessing Michael's—there's a book titled *Beautiful Women, Ugly Scenes.*

The hospital bulletin board, on the other hand, reveals the sort of gallows humor that must be common among the fine men and women of the medical profession. According to today's listings on the board, for example, a Dr. Bendover is scheduled to perform a prostate surgery. It's not all laughs around here though. To set the proper tone, some stickler for details has packed the hospital records room with all sorts of antique medical bills.

Nearby, a few happy *Melrose* set makers can be seen gleefully putting the finishing touches on Amanda's hospital bed for an

Doug Hyun

The cast shares a little dysfunctional holiday cheer during the filming of the 1993 Christmas episode, "Under the Mistletoe."

upcoming scene. With a smile, they report that they've already completed the chemotherapy room. Movingly, when Amanda's sick bed scene gets shot a few days later, Darren Star will visit the set and give Locklear a supportive hug before filming begins.

A short walk from the hospital is the latest addition to these stages—an interior of Michael's beach house. Those looking for hints of scary things to come will want to note that someone's left behind a book here called *Miss Manner's Guide to Rearing Perfect Children*—perhaps some beach reading Kimberly forgot in her haste to leave. Since Michael's always had troubles with family life, it's not too surprising that all the homey photos adorning the beach house turn out to be casual snapshots of various members of the *Melrose* production crew. That's just one more hint that for all the disharmony on screen, *Melrose Place* seems to be one big happy family off the air.

Melrose Imponderables

Why is it that the same people in the exact same formations are often seen in front of the exterior establishing shots in so many episodes?

Where exactly do the residents of 4616 Melrose Place park their cars? And if they live in Los Angeles, how come they don't seem to spend much time in their cars?

Did Billy ever find out that Jake and Alison really did have a night of passion?

Why does Jane keep the Mancini name?

Why the hell do these people stay together?

Grant Show:
Q & A

Much was made during the early days of *Melrose Place* of the mysterious nature of Jake Hanson, the show's strong, silent type transition man in the spinning off from *Beverly Hills, 90210.* As the show's heavily hyped advance man, Show made magazine covers before *Melrose* even premiered. "I think nobody would know how mysterious Jake was if he didn't keep telling people," Grant Show once said of his character. Over the course of three seasons, Jake's opened up and evolved considerably. According to Show, there's been a conscious decision to bring out the heroic side of Jake's persona—think of him as Lancelot with a leather coat and a slight chip on his shoulder. Show made his first splash as Officer Rick Hyde, an angry young man, on the daytime soap *Ryan's Hope.* Eventually, he opted to take time off to study for a year at the London Academy of Music and Dramatic Art. Returning to the States, he did some impressive theater work—including starring as Terry Malloy in an acclaimed Cleveland production of *On the Waterfront*—as well as other television work, before signing on for life as Jake.

Who were the most surprising Melrose Place *fans you've encountered?*

I'm constantly shocked, but the first big surprise had to be all the people on the golf course who stop me. I really didn't expect this show to connect with the older guys on the golf course.

When did you know the show was a hit?

It was the same thing basically. When I started getting preferred tee

Wayne Stambler

117

Jake: A man and his motorcycle.

Timothy White

times because some golf starter was watching *Melrose Place*. And believe me I like those kinds of perks.

What couple that hasn't happened on Melrose *would you like to see?*

Jake and Matt. That would be scary.

Does Melrose Place *give its viewers a sense of warped community?*

I guess we are sort of like one big dysfunctional family. These people stay together, and we don't know why. I mean, I surely wouldn't stay in an apartment complex below some woman with whom I had an affair and then she cheated on me. I wouldn't stay living in a place where I'd slept with one, two, three, four of the women! That's four out of five. By now, I'd be gone!

What's Jake's rent?

Twelve hundred dollars. That's actually what it would be in that part of town, but Jake probably pays about six hundred. Why the hell else would he stay there if the rent's not a bargain? Maybe it's the sex, I guess.

Do you think Jake and Jo will ever work things out in the end?

Yeah, I always play it as if she were the right one—that she's the woman for him—because it's more interesting that way.

Is there anyone from the real world you'd like to see move into Melrose Place*?*

Henry Kissinger.

Do you think Billy and Alison will ever get married? Should they?

Even Jake thinks those two are total lightweights. They'd have to marry each other. Who else is going to take them?

Jake and Jo with Amanda, someone who Jo wishes had taken Jake's "Go Away" welcome mat to heart.

Wayne Stambler

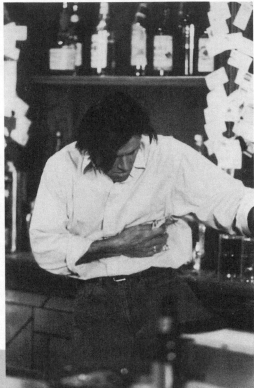

Doug Hyun

It looked like business as usual at Shooters . . .
but a bullet changed all that for Jake.

What's your own favorite Melrose Place *episode?*

One from the first season when Jake found out he had a son. That's probably still my favorite.

How about the least favorite?

That would have to be the time I tore up Jo's refrigerator. That was pretty stupid—who wants to see Jake trashing some refreshments?

Have you ever taken a leisure swim in the pool?

Yeah, sure, I go and do a few laps on my lunch hour. No, I haven't. No one does, probably because we all got so tired of taking our clothes off during the first season.

120

How has Melrose *changed your life?*

Immensely. It's funny because until recently, it really hadn't. I was living in the same house, doing the same things. But all of a sudden, I bought a new house, and it's been totally different. The financial aspects of a job like this are unbelievable. It's not going to go on forever, but I never expected I would have some of the stuff that I have now.

How have things changed behind the scenes at the show over the seasons?

It's become a more efficient machine. We're very professional. I've been on other sets where you go out and drink with everyone after work. This show has never been like that. I guess that every show has its own personality and this one's very businesslike. It's not like people don't like each other. It's just because we have our own lives to take care of.

So do you like Jake?

He's not a bad guy at all. I mean, he grew up without a father and his mother was kind of a 'ho. And whatever mysterious lousy things he did along the way, he never killed anyone. Jake's really trying, you know. Jake's doing just fine.

> "Grant Show is a knockout. Not even loose jeans and a baggy sweater can disguise the goods."
> —Liz Smith, in her column, 1994

Daphne Zuniga: Q & A

If Job—the Bible's leading victim—were an attractive female New York City photographer, perhaps she might look a little something like the endlessly put-upon character Jo Reynolds. Jo moved in during the middle of the first season, and in her debut she copped a lot of major Big Apple attitude. Immediately, she intrigued Billy and Jake, though only the latter would win her already battered heart. Since then, tragically, our Jo has had more than her share of woe. She could write a book called *Smart Woman, Dopey Choices.* So, okay, she had to shoot Reed, the drug-dealing father of her child—get off her back! All of Jo's victimization might get a tad boring were it not played with such finesse by Zuniga, a gifted film actress perhaps best remembered for her starring role opposite John Cusack in Rob Reiner's *The Sure Thing* and for Mel Brooks's *Spaceballs.* Zuniga—an old school friend of Darren Star's from UCLA—admits she had some initial reservations about jumping head first into a television series. "But back then I was frustrated and creatively constipated," she says. "Now I realize that I have the absolute greatest job."

How would you sum up the Melrose Place *philosophy?*

Do what you want, when you want, to whomever you want, because if you don't, your neighbors will.

Does life ever imitate Melrose?

Unfortunately, yes, sometimes (but I haven't shot anyone!).

Wayne Stambler

Any theories on why no one seems to use the pool much anymore?

It's not cleaned enough. No one knows where the pool boy went.

And how come the laundry room was so rarely used for a while there?

Because all of our underwear started disappearing.

What's your favorite line of dialogue you've had on the show so far?

"Jake, I really needed that last night. Thank you."

What about your least favorite?

Same.

Jo and Jake prepare to take a dip in the pool of passion.

Wayne Stambler

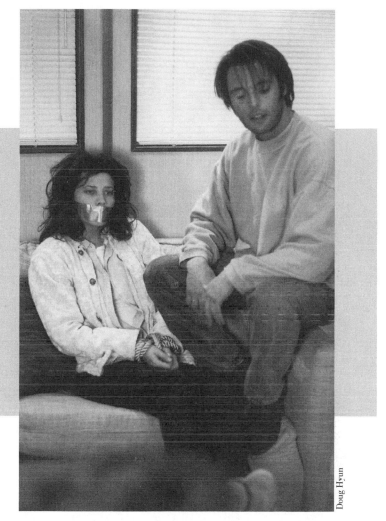

Disturbed, drug-dealing flame Reed tries to work through things with Jo. A bullet and a harpoon took care of him.

Doug Hyun

What couple that hasn't happened yet would you like to see on Melrose?

Jo and Daniel Day-Lewis.

Who from the real world would you like to see move into Melrose Place?

Daniel Day-Lewis . . . oh yeah, and Lassie.

What's the biggest difference between you and your character?

I have more drama in my life!

Jess (Dan Cortese) is yet another chapter in Jo's as-yet-unwritten memoir, *Smart Woman, Dopey Choices.*

Doug Hyun

How has Melrose Place *changed your life?*

I now have a very nice car. And I wake up before the sun does. I thoroughly enjoy playing Jo. I am very grateful to both Aaron and Darren for bringing me into this job. I love going to work! I am very lucky for that!

What's the best outfit you've worn on the show?

The flannel sheets on Jake's bed.

Do you think Jo and Jake will end up together?

I think maybe later in their adult lives. I think that would be a good thing. But they'll both have to flounder a little bit longer. At least two more seasons.

Who's the most surprising Melrose Place *fan you've encountered?*

The drummer of a really big "alternative" band. When he plays, his head flies all over the place. Oh, also a sixty-year-old man told me not to be with Jake because, "He's no good."

What do you think Jo's rent is?

More than she can afford considering she's usually looking for work.

In Reality Bites, *Winona Ryder's character offers the view that* Melrose Place *is a really good show. Why do you think it's a really good show?*

Well, I asked a couple in the yogurt store recently and they told me it's because everyone is evil and sexy.

Ever miss all the bonding of the characters in the first episode?

No . . . boring.

In Jo's first episode she copped a lot of New York attitude. What happened?

I loved that about her. When she first started to go soft I called Darren and said, "Let's not let her go too soft here." But like any character she's going to change. But I love that about her.

What three adjectives best describe Jo?

Bubbly, carefree, hysterically funny.

Does Jo ever miss Sandy and Rhonda?

Never knew Sandy. Rhonda and I still talk—she's very happy. She moved to Beverly Hills.

What do you think Amanda brought to Melrose Place?

Short skirts, goodwill, and messy hair.

What factors made the show survive while so many similar twenty-something shows failed?

Short skirts, goodwill, and messy hair.

What questions do fans ask you the most?

Is the pool real? Is everyone nice? The answer to both is yes.

What do you imagine Jo's favorite album is?

Van Morrison's *Poetic Champions Compose.*

Do you think Alison and Billy will ever *get married? Should they?*

I think I should get a decent partner before they get married!

Which departed Melrose Place *character would you most like to see pay a return visit?*

Not my baby.

So you don't miss Austin personally?

Actually, I kind of do. I'm just happy because logistically it was really tiring, motherhood is tough. It's not because I have anything against infants.

Describe the average Melrose *fan?*

Brilliant.

When did you first know that Melrose Place *was a hit?*

I still don't think I really *know* it.

How have things changed behind the scenes at the show?

We got new dressing rooms that don't leak when it rains. Usually.

What do you think Melrose Place *offers its audience—cheap thrills or a twisted sense of community? Or both?*

Melrose provides one hour a week when fans can appreciate their own lives.

What do you think the tremendous success of Melrose Place *says about Generation X?*

Generation X. What's that? Another Aaron Spelling spin-off?

Doug Savant:
Q & A

According to most *Melrose* insiders, Matt Fielding is probably the best adjusted, most stable, and most civic-minded resident of 4616 Melrose Place. And though too much of Matt's social life has taken place off screen for many of his creators tastes, he nonetheless remains a groundbreaking character in television his-

Dana Fineman

Timothy White

Until she moved away, Rhonda was Matt's best friend.

tory. In a building of heterosexual nut jobs, Matt is a sympathetic, even heroic presence. Since the beginning, Doug Savant has lent Matt a quiet but powerful dignity, even back in those days during the first season when it seemed as if he had little to do of dramatic consequence besides serving as Rhonda's personal cheerleader. Before *Melrose Place*, Savant was seen starring opposite Rob Lowe in the film *Masquerade* and as an American P.O.W. in *The Hanoi Hilton*. "The truth is I'm incredibly fortunate to be working on this show," says Savant, "especially considering before this I was back to delivering pizzas at Dino's Pizza in Burbank for four dollars and seventy-five cents an hour."

When did you first know that Melrose Place *was a hit?*

When journalists began asking me my opinion regarding matters of public policy, I began to realize the show must be a hit. Why else would anyone be interested in printing the opinions of a guy who only a few minutes earlier was delivering pizzas?

Who is the most surprising fan of the show that you've ever encountered?

While standing at the baggage claim in the Colorado Springs airport, I was approached by a fan who wanted to introduce me to his girlfriend. As is common etiquette, after introducing myself, the man introduced himself to me. That man's name: John Wayne Bobbitt.

Timothy White

Why is it that no one goes into the laundry room much anymore?

Often I am asked why Matt isn't more involved in many of the episodes of *Melrose Place.* Please know that when Matt isn't present in a scene, he's busy doing the laundry of the other tenants. If you don't see Matt, that means he's fluffing and folding for Amanda and Jake.

What a nice guy. Do you think Matt has a dark side?

Absolutely. We'll just never see it. Matt is the conscience of *Melrose Place* and I think the audience roots for him because of that. I have, however, dreamed up some wonderfully bizarre and unexpected ways to reveal Matt's as yet unseen dark side. I picture a courtyard scene where Jake and Amanda, rekindling their

A rare guilty look from Matt.

Doug Hyun

romantic spark, are interrupted as Sigfried and Roy with a white tiger exit Matt's apartment. Or perhaps as a scene is being played out in one of the other apartments we become aware of the sounds of *Phantom of the Opera* coming from Matt's apartment. Cut to Matt's apartment where he is seen in black mask and cape running hither and yon singing at the top of his lungs "The Phantom of the Opera."

So would that be Matt's favorite album?

No, that would be *Simply Barbra.*

In the pilot of the show, Matt remarked to Rhonda that Billy was cute. Do you think Matt still finds any of the men of Melrose *attractive?*

I think initially Matt felt that Billy was indeed cute and had a great deal of potential, but Jake now has a burgeoning sensitivity that places him above Billy on the "Most Attractive Tenant" list for Matt. Jake, having always possessed a large yang, is now getting in touch with his yin, and that balance is what attracts Matt. Add to the above that on occasion I have been mistaken for Grant Show, and it crosses over into some twisted narcissistic attraction that appeals to me.

Any guesses on why nobody on the show seems to use the pool much anymore?

My theory is that Amanda is pretty picky about the amount of scum in the pool, so she doesn't allow any of the tenants to actually use it anymore.

How have things changed behind the scenes at Melrose Place*?*

From the point of view of the actors, things have loosened up considerably. By necessity, everyone's become facile at going with whatever's present in the script. The whole show has become a well-oiled machine. And the people who are most responsible for that are the crew who—unlike the actors—are here all day, every day doing the hardest work.

Do you have a favorite episode?

I have a sense of pride for the Christmas episode of the second season in which Matt put Nikki—who was played by the great Mara

Wilson—on a plane to Russia and had to say good-bye to her. What was special was the chance to show that Matt, an openly gay man, still has an incredibly strong pull toward having a traditional family, and that he has a deep sense of family and tremendous love for a child. I thought that was important.

Have you ever attended a Melrose Place *viewing party?*

Never. The closest I've come was the first time I accessed America Online. I found the entertainment section and figured I'd listen in on what people have to say about the show. I pulled up something called "MP Party," and someone there was writing about me! That was bizarre, another chapter of absurdity in the life of Doug Savant.

What's the biggest difference between you and Matt?

Actually, I'm . . . taller.

The Wit and Wisdom of Melrose Place

This chapter, which could be subtitled "The World According to *Melrose*," is dedicated to collecting just a partial sampling of the vast wit and wisdom that has sprung forth from *Melrose Place*. Think of this as "the quotable *Melrose*," a useful and trashy reference resource for *Melrose* obsessives. It is this author's moderately humble hope that these words—these teachings, if you will—will be a valuable source of knowledge, pleasure, and solace to all who seek the word of *Melrose*. As it turns out, there are not many big questions or issues in life that the show has not managed to address over three seasons spent in the dogged pursuit of truth, knowledge, and a demographically

Wayne Stambler

135

attractive audience. Thus the following insights represent a veritable users' guide to living a Melrosian life. These quotes come from the scripts for all three seasons of the series as well as from interviews and reviews related to *Melrose Place*.

On God

"Sydney, you are looking at human garbage who would have run you over as soon as look at you. When Michael's dead, God's going to do a jig."

—Kimberly soliciting Sydney as her partner-in-crime in "Till Death Do Us Part," 1994

On the Distinction Between Art and Life

This officially confirms that I have met Thomas Calabro of Melrose Place, *and he's a hell of a lot nicer than the guy he plays on TV.*

—A business card handed out to fans by Thomas Calabro, who plays bad guy, Michael Mancini

On Friendship

"Here's your bridesmaid's dress. Give it to a friend—if you have one left."

—Amanda regretfully declining Alison's invitation to be in her wedding party in "Till Death Do Us Part," 1994

"Just remember, friends do it too."

—Explosive love interest Brittany Maddocks's friendly come-on to Jake in "I Am Curious, Melrose," 1994

Kathy Ireland as Brittany Maddocks.

Andrew Semel

"Count your friends, Michael. Oops. Done already?"
—Amanda mocking Michael in "Framing of the Shrews," 1995

On Good Versus Evil

"Amanda's not that bad. Her heart does beat on occasion, but then it just stops."
—Heather Locklear, to Margy Rochlin in *Rolling Stone*, 1994

"It's fun playing the bad one. Bad characters get to dance on tables and say the last line and leave the room while the other person crumbles. Things I wouldn't do in real life."
—Heather Locklear, to Margy Rochlin in *Mademoiselle*, 1993

MICHAEL: *You decent?*
AMANDA: *That's a matter of opinion.*
—A revealing moment of hospital humor from
"St. Valentine's Day Massacre," 1995

On Moral Dilemmas

"I hate moral dilemmas."
—Jake figuring out what to do about his relationship with
Kelly Taylor in the pilot episode, 1992

On Lifestyle Choices

MATT: *How can you stay with a woman who tries to kill you?*
MICHAEL: *Do I judge your lifestyle, Matt?*
—Matt and Michael ask dueling questions in
"Nonsexual Healing," 1994

On Family Values

"I just worry that, you know, your life is a little too complicated for me. I mean, it's tough enough being gay without a wife and kid to worry about."
—Art gallery owner Joel Walker explaining why Matt's life might be
a tad too complicated for his tastes in "Married to It," 1993

"Please tell me you'll always be daddy's little girl . . . I love you, pumpkin. More than anybody."
—The child-molesting Mr. Parker's creepy prewedding comments to Alison in "Till Death Do Us Part," 1994

MR. PARKER: *You two, you've grown up so healthy.*
MEREDITH: *You call this healthy? I have a gun on you. And my baby sister is jumping out of windows on her wedding day. We are a mess.*
—A heart-tugging father-daughter chat in "I Am Curious, Melrose," 1994

On Playing Doctor

MICHAEL: *You sure you don't need a physical while you're here?*
AMANDA: *Keep your stethoscope in your pocket, Doctor.*
—A frisky hospital exchange from "In Bed with the Enemy," 1994

Diego Uchitel

On Marriage as an Institution

"Are you insinuating I'm not fulfilling my husbandly duties?"
—Michael to his neglected wife Jane, shortly after she has kissed his toes in the pilot episode, 1992

"Something in the back of my mind told me if we don't spend some quality time together soon, we're going to be headed for trouble."
—Jane showing great foresight in the pilot episode, 1992

"I could never do anything to hurt you. I love you sweetheart. You're my angel."
> —Michael reassuring Jane as their marriage
> collapses in "Carpe Diem," 1993

JANE: *I'm sorry. I've been so distracted lately.*
JO: *It's PMS—postmarriage syndrome.*
> —Jo offers the new divorcée an expert diagnosis in
> "Fire Power," 1993

"You don't need my blessing, Sydney, you need serious psychological attention."
> —Jane offering a moment of sisterly advice regarding Syd's impend-
> ing nuptials to Michael in "Otherwise Engaged," 1994

SYDNEY: *Please, Michael, we're married. I'm your wife.*
MICHAEL: *No, you are my ex-wife. Now back off before I run over your toes accidentally.*
> —The Mancinis working things out in "Imperfect Strangers," 1994

"Let me ask you a question you might run into on the test, just to see how you'd do. If you were mad at your husband would you (a) con-front him, (b) cheat on him, or (c) dress up as someone else and run over him."
> —Michael helping Kimberly prep for a psychological test in
> "Another Perfect Day in Hell," 1995

On Revenge

"My first instinct was to fire you as well. But on reflection, I realized that was way too easy. No, Alison, I'm going to do you the way you did me. And when I'm done, all that you'll be left with is that prover-bial wish—that you'd never been born."
> —Amanda interfacing with her favorite employee, Alison, in
> "Devil with the G-String On," 1994

On Premarital Bliss

SYDNEY: *We're perfect for each other. Don't you get it?*
MICHAEL: *Get this, Sydney, you are one stupid slut who's crossed the*

line, and I don't want to see your face anymore.
SYDNEY: *Jane warned me about how cranky you get in the morning.*
—Some prewedding jitters from "Otherwise Engaged," 1994

On the Trouble with House Guests

"I thought I could stay with you guys till I get my act together."
—Sydney to the Mancinis in "Single White Sister," 1993

"I'm here Jane. I'm here to stay."
—Sydney to her beloved sister in "Single White Sister," 1993. By
the very next episode, "Peanut Butter and Jealousy," Jane
has a nightmare about Michael and Sydney having an affair.

On Not Loving Thy Neighbor

*"I have really had it with all the petty garbage around here—all of
you. You keep rehashing it. You sling it from one apartment to the
next. You know self-absorption is a bottomless pit in this place."*
—Jake, on living in the world's most complex apartment complex in
"Nonsexual Healing," 1994

On Justice and Dieting

*"We'll be out to lunch and Heather will say, 'Yes, I'd like fried zuc-
chini circles with ranch.' And I'll be having a tuna salad with fat-free
dressing. I hate her."*
—Courtney Thorne-Smith joking about her castmate,
quoted in *TV Guide,* 1994

*"I'm naturally thin. But the older I get . . . my butt's becoming part of
my leg."*
—Heather Locklear, quoted in *People,* 1994

On Suspicion

*"Why is it every time a girl doesn't show up at night, people think
she's at my apartment?"*
—Jake taking offense in the pilot episode, 1992

On Paying the Rent

"I've heard that it's between six and eight hundred dollars, which is actually pretty reasonable. I mean, it's a really cute place with a pool and lots of action. When I was in college, a two-bedroom in Westwood was twelve hundred a month, and that was some time ago."

—Heather Locklear no doubt laying the groundwork
for Amanda's future rent hike, 1994

"I think they're about eight hundred for a one bedroom, twelve hundred for a two bedroom. Maybe they've gone up a little since we established them, because the place is looking a little nicer."

—Darren Star, 1994

On Monogamy

"I believe in being faithful."

—Michael rejecting Sydney during a brief episode of
memory loss in "Grand Delusions," 1994

On Tabloids

"They've had me pregnant a million times. They've had me anorexic. They've called me everything but a bitch. Only Melrose Place *can do that."*

—Heather Locklear talking about trashy journalists,
quoted in *TV Guide,* 1995

On the Absurdity of Gender Politics

MATT: *He's cute.*
RHONDA: *Don't even think about it. I saw him first.*

—The best of friends discussing new arrival Billy in
the pilot episode, 1992

"If you're going to kiss me, don't do that pent-up macho anger thing. I don't like bruises."

—Amanda expressing her preferences to Jake in
"No Bed of Roses," 1993

"Our subject is 'women who can't get enough.'"
> —Dr. Ruth Westheimer appearing in Billy's dream sequence in
> "Friends and Lovers," 1992

SANDY: *I'm just looking for a little compassion.*
JAKE: *Sorry, wrong gender.*
> —The former lovers duke it out in
> "My Way," 1992

On Beefcake and Cheesecake

"A little of that will help a show, and a lot can hurt it. We walk that line. But the truth of the matter is that we're a glam show, and part of what we're selling is sex."
> —Grant Show, 1994

"Am I sensitive beefcake? Hmm, that's interesting. What exactly is beefcake? Does it taste good."
> —Andrew Shue, 1994

On Sensitive Men

"Think about it. I am a great guy. I'm smart, talented. I listen. How many guys do you know who are as sensitive as me?"
> —Billy blowing his own horn to Alison in
> "Swept Away," 1994

BILLY: *She means everything to me. And losing her will make everything else in my life insignificant.*
GREG: *I thought that was the kind of mush you only heard in chick movies.*
> —Billy returning to sappy form to his *Escapade* coworker in
> "Swept Away," 1994

On Orgasm

"I think I finally understand what Meg Ryan was faking in When Harry Met Sally.*"*
> —Alison explaining to Jane the outcome of her first time
> in bed with future sicko Keith in "Polluted Affair," 1993

On Self-Improvement

AMANDA: *I just think sometimes I'm a little too blunt with people and I should work on that.*
JO: *Couldn't hurt.*
　—Amanda makes a breakthrough in "Long Night's Journey," 1993

On the Social Significance of *Melrose Place*

"Do they pay you a lot of money to make you ask a question like that?"
—Grant Show, asked to address the message of *Melrose,*
quoted in *Rolling Stone,* 1994

"Does the show have social significance? Hmm . . . I'd have to say no."
Daphne Zuniga, 1994

On Trial Separations

SYDNEY: *It looks like the Sleaze Bag Hall of Fame is missing a member. Now what would bring vermin like you out in the daylight? I know, you want to apologize.*
MICHAEL: *No, Syd, I want a divorce.*
SYDNEY: *And I want to wake up tomorrow morning and sing like Aretha Franklin. Do the words, "go to hell" mean anything to you?*
—Sydney and Michael try to work through their troubles in "Nonsexual Healing," 1994

On Motherhood

"You're uptight, you're high-strung, you're overjudgmental—My God, it would be like living with my mother."
—Billy to Alison in the pilot episode, 1992

"Mom, do me a favor. Get back on your broom and fly back to Chicago."
—Sydney letting her mother know she doesn't have to stick around for her wedding to Michael in "Otherwise Engaged," 1994

Wayne Stambler

"You're not Mrs. Mancini. There's only one Mrs. Mancini, and that's my damned mother."
—Michael setting the record straight to Sydney in "With This Ball and Chain," 1994

On Fatherhood

"I wish I'd never had either of you. I wish you'd never been born."
—Mr. Parker opens up to his daughters in "It's a Bad World After All," 1994

On the Media

"I'm actually going to cancel the paper—it's just more proof that the world sucks."
—Jo comments on the importance of keeping up with current events in "Another Perfect Day in Hell," 1995

On the Swimming Pool

"I once said that part of my deal here was that I'd never have to get in the pool, because I'm over thirty. Now they say they want to see an over-thirty body in a bathing suit, which is sweet, I guess."
—Heather Locklear, quoted in *Rolling Stone,* 1994

"Early on we took a drubbing from the critics about everybody always jumping in and out of the pool. We got a little gun-shy about using the pool."
—Darren Star, 1994

On *The Brady Bunch*

"I did not spend four years in medical school and two in residency to become Carol Brady. And even she had Alice to help around the house."
—Kimberly in "Revenge," 1993

On Cults

"Adios, you fruitcakes."
—Sydney's parting words to the members of the Abbot Way cult in
"St. Valentine's Day Massacre," 1995

On Warfare

*"You can't for a minute believe that Kimberly is helpless. If they had
to invade Normandy again, they'd put her in charge."*
—Sydney comparing Kimberly with Dwight D. Eisenhower in
"Nonsexual Healing," 1994

On the Power of Understatement

"We have a very odd relationship."
—Alison's insightful reaction when Billy gives Alison a condom
before she goes off to sleep with Keith for the first time in
"Polluted Affair," 1992

On the Advantages of Small Weddings

*"I hate most of my relatives anyway, and besides they were all at your
wedding with June, so there's no way they would come. I mean it
would be like seeing a remake of a movie that's only a few years old."*
—Sydney explaining her preference for an intimate affair to Michael
in "Otherwise Engaged," 1994

On Generation X

*"This generation gets a really bad rap, I think. They just don't want
to screw up. They don't want to make the wrong choices."*
—Andrew Shue, 1995

"On Melrose Place *we have tons of problems, but most of them seem
pretty self-created. My friends in their twenties are trying to take control
of their lives. On* Melrose Place, *we just kind of let things happen to us."*
—Courtney Thorne-Smith, 1995

"I think a true Generation X show would be about eight characters sitting around with no jobs and lots of time on their hands. That would get pretty dull pretty quickly. These characters are not slackers."

—Darren Star, 1994

On Ecology

"He's not an ax murderer. He's an ecologist, and a pretty wimpy one at that."

—Alison about her soon-to-be psycho boy toy Keith in "Long Night's Journey," 1993

On Happiness Being Boring

"Viewers always say, 'Gee, can't they all be happy?' But the show would be very dull if they were happy. It's really tough to write scenes of happy couples cooing at each other. It gets dull real fast, so we have to keep throwing them curves."

—Darren Star, 1994

On the Agony of Heartbreak

JAKE: *Well, Jo and me are a done deal.*
BILLY: *It's not over till the fat lady sings.*
JAKE: *Not only has the fat lady sung, she's taken her bows, gone home, and she's in bed asleep right about now.*

—Jake and Billy's beer-drenched poolside heart-to-heart in "Of Bikes and Men," 1993

On the Sting of Rejection

SYDNEY: *Please don't make me wait.*
MICHAEL: *If you think I'm making love to you, you're going to be waiting a long time.*
SYDNEY: *Is that your game, Michael. You want me to beg?*
MICHAEL: *Beg? Hell, bark for all I care. I wouldn't sleep with you at gun point.*

—Michael letting Sydney down easy in "Grand Delusions," 1994

On Location, Location, Location

"There's a certain sensuality in closer proximity. I remember when Darren and I talked about this crazy idea of having Heather buy the apartment building. I remembered this expression used in a play—it must have been Noel Coward. The line was 'That puts the cat among the pigeons, doesn't it?' I think that had a tremendous impact."

> —Aaron Spelling, quoted in
> *Rolling Stone,* 1994

On Bitchiness

ALISON: *I know I've been a bit of a bitch since I got home.*
BILLY: *No more than usual.*

> —The apartment mates mix it up in *"Melrose Place Christmas,"* 1992

Diego Uchitel

On Getting Along with the In-Laws

"Michael, you're so cool to be with. Look, I know you and I haven't been total buds, but I thought, you know, this trip could bring us a little closer."

> —Michael's sister-in-law and future wife, Sydney, reaches out to him in her first appearance in "Single White Sister," 1993

"I just want her to be happy, but come on. My job, my apartment, what's next—you?"

> —Jane to Michael about Sydney in "Single White Sister," 1993

"No matter what, I'll always love Jane. Hell, I'll love the whole family."

> —Michael comforting Sydney in "Long Night's Journey," 1993

MR. CARTER: *You didn't think we'd allow our only grandchild to be raised by a cold-blooded killer?*
JO: *This is obviously a mistake.*

147

MRS. CARTER: *You seem to make a lot of those, dear.*
——Jo bonding badly with Reed's folks in "Grand Delusions," 1994

On Rules of Engagement

SYDNEY: *Neutral territories do not have king-sized beds in the middle of them.*
MICHAEL: *It's neutral until the first shot is fired.*
——The estranged couple try to negotiate peace with dignity in "Nonsexual Healing," 1994

"And for the record, I'd never accept anything less than three carats."
——Amanda offering one more reason for rejecting Michael's marriage proposal in "All About Brooke," 1995

On Literary Aesthetics

"So what exactly is a literary aesthetic?"
——Jane making party chatter in "Another Perfect Day in Hell," 1995

On the Thin Line Between Love and Hate

JAKE: *One minute you're ready to evict me, the next minute you want to . . .*
AMANDA: *Practically rape you? Call me unpredictable.*
——Jake and Amanda enjoying the irony in "Michael's Game," 1994

On Dealing with Subordinates

"Over here, rocket butt . . . Guns n' Roses makes you impotent."
——Amanda talking to a lowly office messenger in her first episode, "Picture Imperfect," 1993

On Interoffice Relations

CHRIS MARCHETTE: *Tell me, what's your policy regarding kissing at the office?*

JANE: *Extremely progressive.*
—Things getting hot and heavy at Mancini Designs in "In-Laws and Outlaws," 1994

On Office Politics

ALISON: *Love the Miss Congeniality act.*
BILLY: *I don't think Amanda's acting. I think she's just sincere in wanting to get back to work.*
ALISON: *More like she saw an opportunity to slip rat poison in my latte.*
—Alison reacting to Amanda's offer to get coffee for everyone in "All About Brooke," 1995

On Big Business

"What can I say—when God was passing out business sense Jane was in the back of the line getting her nails done."
—Amanda assessing the savvy of Jane to Michael in "Dr. Jeckyl Saves His Hide," 1994

"Blackmail is a growth industry."
—Sydney giving Jane a business tip in "Melrose Impossible," 1995

On Literature

BILLY: *I'm a writer.*
ALISON: *You mean like Jackie Collins.*
BILLY: *No, like Norman Mailer.*
—Billy and Alison splitting hairs in the pilot episode, 1992

BILLY: *I'm a writer.*
JO: *Oh, really, I didn't know there were any real writers in L.A.*
BILLY: *Oh God, not that attitude. I'm so sick of hearing that.*
—Billy trying to get to know Jo in "House of God," 1992

Andrew Semel

"My fantasy is to go to Europe and become an ex-patriot writer, and spend a decade on a great novel—Fitzgerald without the elitist self-destruction, or Hemingway without the guns, or Joyce without the sexual guilt."

—Billy staking out his literary turf to Amanda in "Three's a Crowd," 1993

On Ernest Hemingway in Particular

"At my age Hemingway was already in Africa shooting elephants. Real writers do things, you know. They get into barroom brawls, and go through women like Kleenex. They have terrible drinking problems. They destroy their lives and everyone they care about. Come on, we're going to Shooters. I can at least start working on my drinking problem."

—Billy torturing himself in "Leap of Faith," 1992

On the Relative Merits of Emily Dickinson

ALISON: *Nobody said you had to drink to be a writer. No one even said you had to have adventures. Look at Emily Dickinson. She hardly even left her house.*
BILLY: *What a candy-ass!*

—Another lively literary debate from "Leap of Faith," 1992

On Literary Failure

"I'm a sucker for Viking funerals."

—Billy's explanation to Alison as he barbecues his failed screenplay, *The Big Shock*, in "Lost and Found," 1992

On Chemistry

"A class I failed."

—Grant Show when asked to define the term *chemistry*, quoted in *Us* magazine, 1994

On Barry Manilow

JAKE: *Did they still call you "Mandy" in college?*
AMANDA: *Don't ever call me that.*
JAKE: *What's wrong with "Mandy"? It was good enough for Barry Manilow.*
> —Jake pestering Amanda about her childhood nickname in "The Tangled Web," 1993

On the Actor's Life

"I studied at the Actors' Circle and six months with Reilly, Charles Nelson Reilly."
> —Sandy impressing *Beverly Hills, 90210*'s Steve Sanders in the *Melrose Place* pilot episode, 1992

"I'm just lucky that I have one of those great roles where I get paid well to be incredibly obnoxious."
> —Laura Leighton, quoted in *Rolling Stone*, 1994

On Forgiveness

MICHAEL: *Can't we be friends? I know a lot of bad things have happened, but that's water under the bridge now.*
JANE: *So much water there's not much of a bridge left, Michael.*
> —The former spouses hashing it out one more time in "Collision Course," 1993

ALISON: *You could be a little more understanding.*
AMANDA: *I could be a lot more understanding, but where would that get me?*
> —A typically warm exchange from "Devil with the G-String On," 1994

On the Lost Art of Conversation

"If I wanted conversation I'd call a nine-hundred line."
> —Jake getting things straight with Amanda in "Flirting with Disaster," 1993

On Gays on TV

"I've never made a comment about my sexuality publicly. . . . Andrew Shue outed me as straight in People *magazine. While I would like Matt's character to have more teeth, he's definitely a good, ethical guy. Somebody has to wear the white hat in the show, and it might as well be the gay character."*

—Doug Savant, quoted in *The Advocate,* 1994

"Oh my God."
   —Billy's reaction to seeing Matt kiss his old college buddy Rob in "Till Death Do Us Part, 1994

BILLY: *Were you ever attracted to me?*
ROB: *No.*
BILLY: *Why not?*
ROB: *I don't know, Billy. I guess I was looking for someone a little more stable.*
   —Billy and his pal getting past matters of sexual preference in "Till Death Do Us Part," 1994

On Hate Crimes

KIMBERLY: *Broken ribs. Hmm, I'm surprised. I told them to break your arm.*
MATT: *Don't try and take credit for this. You had nothing to do with this. It was a hate crime.*
KIMBERLY: *You bet your butt it was. I hate you.*
   —Kimberly displays her bedside manner in "Another Perfect Day in Hell," 1995

On the Don't Ask, Don't Tell Policy

JEFFREY: *U.S. Navy and gay? Not exactly compatible terms.*
MATT: *Yeah, what about the "Don't ask, don't tell policy"?*
JEFFREY: *It'll work maybe in ten years, but navy regulations aren't nearly as brutal as my family's. My father's a retired vice admiral, and his policy is just "don't." Period.*
   —A ripped-from-the-headlines conversation from "Arousing Suspicion," 1994

On the Art of the Putdown

KIMBERLY: *Matt, you're pathetic.*
MATT: *And your . . . wig is crooked.*
> —A fond chat from "Boxing Sydney," 1995

On Love Scenes

"Feeding a guy strawberries in bed is never easy."
> —Heather Locklear, quoted in *TV Guide*, 1993

On TV as a Catharsis

"What we're saying is, don't do it. We're your outlet. We've done it so you don't have to."
> —Thomas Calabro, quoted in *Rolling Stone*, 1994

On Abstinence

JAKE: *You know what they say—abstinence makes the heart grow fonder.*
SANDY: *That's absence.*
JAKE: *Whatever.*
> —From "Responsibly Yours," 1992

Timothy White

On Abortion

"I think you're making a really complicated choice here. We're not talking about returning a dress."
> —Jake's family-planning advice to Jo in "Otherwise Engaged," 1994

On Faux Pas

"Kimberly and I made a baby together . . . I mean delivered a baby together."
>—Michael misspeaks in *"Melrose Place* Christmas," 1992

On Fashion Sense

"Personally, I've never understood the virtue of packing lightly, or maybe I just don't have your flair for making one outfit work three different ways."
>—Amanda's backhanded compliment to Alison during their
>weekend trip in "Carpe Diem," 1993

"It's my skirts that do all the acting."
>—Heather Locklear being humble, quoted in *Vanity Fair,* 1994

On Arranged Marriages

"We have an arrangement. I buy you furniture, and you annoy me as little as possible."
>—Michael explaining matrimony to Sydney in
>"In Bed with the Enemy," 1994

On High Finance

"Billy's like that company you bought in St. Louis. He's an undervalued asset. And with the right management he can be a Fortune 500 company in no time."
>—The ambitious Brooke Armstrong giving the prospectus on Billy
>to her rich daddy Hayley in "The Big Bang Theory," 1995

On Community

"Welcome, it's a pretty nice building. The natives are a little weird, but they're friendly."
>—Then building manager Michael greeting Billy
>in the pilot episode, 1992

Diego Uchitel

MARCY: *It's just so cool how all of you know each other. In my building we're all strangers.*
MATT: *We all look out for each other.*
MARCY: *Kind of like a family.*
MATT: *Exactly.*
> —A poolside chat between Matt and one of Billy's one-episode stands in "Friends and Lovers," 1992

SYDNEY: *The other tenants can be a little nosy and the landlord is a real wench.*
RIKKI: *I can deal with people like that real easy. Any cute guys?*
SYDNEY: *A few.*
RIKKI: *Good, 'cause they're essential to the mix.*
> —Syd and her cult-loving prospective roommate consider the complex in "They Shoot Mothers Don't They?" 1995

On Law and Order

"Pay your rent on time. You never knock on this door before eight A.M. unless it's an emergency, don't pee in the pool."
> —Michael lays down the law of the complex to Billy in
> the pilot episode, 1992

On Criminal Justice

SYDNEY: *I'm a designer too, you know. I'm not just working for Jane to satisfy some silly court-order probation.*
AMANDA: *And to think your talents might have been wasted making license plates in some women's prison.*
> —A typically supportive exchange from "The Cook, the Creep, His
> Lover, and Her Sister," 1994

"This is not Iraq, man. She's got rights."
> —Legal scholar Jake arguing with the authorities on Jo's behalf
> after she's harpooned and shot Reed to death in
> "With This Ball and Chain," 1994

On Bicoastal Tensions

"If all you people from New York hate Los Angeles so much, why do you all move out here?"
> —Billy hitting Jo a profound question in her first episode,
> "House of God," 1992

"At least in L.A. they say, 'Have a nice day' after they've been rude to you."
> —Billy's pet peeve about the Big Apple in
> "Parting Glances," 1994

"This is New York. We eat worms like you for breakfast. Now be a good little Angeleno and leave. Vaya Con Dios."
> —A surly receptionist at Dr. Steele's office putting Michael in his
> place in "Breakfast at Tiffany's, Dinner at Eight," 1995

On Curious Medical Come-Ons

"So I'm just another lymphoma to you?"
—Ailing Amanda's comment to Michael in "Boxing Sydney," 1995

"If you ever think of dying again, I'll kill you."
—Amanda comforting a hospitalized Jake in
"Framing of the Shrews, 1995

On the Drug Problem

JAKE: *I don't do that crap anymore.*
PERRY: *You're so 1990s.*
—Jake rejecting his coke-snorting, modern art-dealing ex-flame
Perry in "For Love or Money," 1992

"This could be thirtysomething *on an Ecstasy rush."*
—Matt Roush on *Melrose Place*, in *USA Today*, 1992

On Relationships

*"I know I'm a naive nitwit from the Midwest, but are all relationships
in L.A. this haphazard and ridiculous?"*
—Alison in "Friends and Lovers," 1992

*"He's not my boyfriend. We need T-shirts that say, 'We're platonic, we
swear.'"*
—Alison talking about her arrangement with her roommate Billy in
"Three's a Crowd," 1993

*"Why do I have this feeling that you two are married, and neither one
wants to admit it?"*
—Amanda in "Three's a Crowd," 1993

SYDNEY: *Michael, I love you.*
MICHAEL: *Well, that's your problem, isn't it?*
—A touching exchange from "Married to It," 1993

"That's the problem, Syd. Blackmail isn't a very good building block for a relationship."

> —Jane offering her kid sister some solid advice in "The Bitch Is Back," 1994

"Excuse me, is it just my imagination or were we supposed to be having a relationship?"

> —Amanda confronting the wavering, Jo-bound Jake in "Till Death Do Us Part," 1994

On Increasing Incidents of Death Among Love Interests of *Melrose Place* Cast Members

"Are we rough on our boyfriends or what?"

> —Jo female-bonding with her pal Alison in "Love, Mancini Style," 1994

On the Importance of Communication

"We've got to talk."

—Jake's favorite breakup words spoken in the same episode to both Amanda and Jo, "Till Death Do Us Part," 1994

On Mental Health

JANE: *How are you, Sydney?*
SYDNEY: *Fabulous, Jane! Couldn't be better. I love this place. It's like summer camp with electroshock therapy.*

> —Sydney offering her review of the sanitarium in "In-Laws and Outlaws," 1994

"When was the last time you took a mental health day?"

> —Alison's music industry weasel boyfriend, Zack Phillips, suggesting making more time to party in "The Days of Wine and Vodka," 1994

On Codependency

BILLY: *You're a classic codependent.*
ALISON: *Who made you the expert?*
BILLY: *You did.*

—Billy shrink-raps his ex in "They Shoot
Mothers Don't They?" 1995

On Being Fab

"If we're the Beatles, does that make me Ringo?"
—Doug Savant, quoted in *Entertainment Weekly*, 1994

On Sadomasochistic Tendencies

"Kill me or love me. You make up your mind."
Michael to Kimberly who seems to have turned him on by
attempting to kill him in "Grand Delusions," 1994

On the Unreliability of First Impressions

"She's terrific. I haven't made a friend like that at work in a while."
—Amanda to Billy about her new pal Alison in
"Three's a Crowd," 1993

On Infidelity

JANE: *I just wanted to tell you I think you are disgusting. I only hope that someday if you're ever lucky enough to find a man of your own that some pathetic bitch will come along and hurt you the way you hurt me.*
KIMBERLY: *Jane, it's not over.*
JANE: *I'm getting a divorce.*

—Jane's and Kimberly's show-
down at Wilshire Memorial in
"Suspicious Minds," 1993

Diego Uchitel

On the Passage of Time

"I can't play a twenty-five-year-old for the rest of my life. It seems like I've been doing it for seventy-five years already."
—Heather Locklear, quoted in *TV Guide*, 1992

On the Night Life

"Daytime is just a dress rehearsal."
—The not-long-for-the-series Sandy giving her philosophy in the pilot episode, 1992

On Being a Man of Mystery

JAKE: *Kelly, I've got problems you don't even know about.*
KELLY TAYLOR: *You know Dylan was right about one thing. He said you have a great heart, but you didn't know how to open it up.*
—Jake and a besotted Kelly Taylor having it out in the pilot episode, 1992

"I'm always pissed off about something, aren't I?"
—Jake to Colleen, the mother of his son, David, in "Jake Versus Jake," 1992

JO: *He may not show you how much he loves you.*
JESS: *Cut the crap, lady. I know all about the Clint Eastwood act. I use it myself.*
—Jess discussing his brother Jake with Jo in "Love and Death 101," 1995

On Politics

"It's pretty surprising how many people running our country watch my show."
—Daphne Zuniga after attending the eightieth annual White House Correspondents' Association Dinner, quoted in *TV Guide*, 1994

On Political Correctness

"Will you please call off Shamu, the politically correct whale?"
—Billy making fun of Alison's earnest but not yet psychotic love interest Keith in "My New Partner," 1993

On Swimwear

"What's with all these pool scenes? I showed up on the set one day, and she's wearing dental floss!"
—Rob Estes, husband of Josie Bissett and star of *Silk Stalkings*, on his wife's pool appearances, quoted in *People*, 1992

On Sex

JAKE: *Did you have a good time last night?*
JO: *Which time?*
—The new couple the morning after their first night together in "Three's a Crowd," 1993

On Pajamas

BILLY: *To tell you the truth, all the girls I've slept with either wore T-shirts or football jerseys to bed.*
AMANDA: *You're with a woman now.*
BILLY: *It's about time.*
—Billy and Amanda getting ready for bed the first time in "My New Partner," 1993

On Underwear

"I don't wear underwear."
—Thomas Calabro, quoted in *Entertainment Weekly*, 1994

On Wedding Wear

SYDNEY: *You ruined Grandma's dress!*
JANE: *On the contrary, Syd, now it's tailor-made for the bride of Frankenstein.*

> —A sisterly moment following the watery catfight in "Otherwise Engaged," 1994

On Dressing for Success

"If Amanda wants to wear the pants at the agency, she should wear some pants to the agency."

> —Sharon Hall, an ad woman at BBDO, on Amanda's sartorial style, quoted in *Glamour,* 1994

"A tie? You've got to be kidding me. This is Los Angeles! Enjoy your dinner, Amanda. I stay out of clubs that would never have me for a member."

> —Jake "Groucho" Hanson reacting to the dress requirements of a stuffy restaurant in "Devil with the G-String On," 1994

On the Christmas Spirit

"Can't you let the weight of the world off your shoulders and have one cup of eggnog with me?"

> —An early seasonal come-on by Kimberly to Michael in *"Melrose Place* Christmas," 1992

"You play your cards right now you might get lucky before New Year's—maybe Valentine's Day."

> —Jo's holiday sweet talk to Jake in *"Melrose Place* Christmas," 1992

On the Joy of Sex

"I feel like I'm having my own private bed-a-thon, with all the donations coming to me."

> —Jo bragging to Jane about her love affair with Jake's brother Jess in "Hose by Any Other Name," 1995

On Being Misunderstood

AMANDA: *Why is it when you try to help one person you end up getting stepped on by another?*
JAKE: *You know what your problem is—you're misunderstood.*
AMANDA: *Darn right.*
> —Jake sounding a familiar theme in "Married to It," 1993

On the Pain of Love

"Love hurts. Remember that, Michael."
> —Kimberly's vivid reminder after she intentionally bites Michael's lip and draws blood in "To Live and Die in Malibu," 1995

On Bonding

"There's nobody I don't like. Maybe in six years it will be different."
> —Courtney Thorne-Smith on relations with her new castmates, quoted in *USA Today*, 1992

On Castration Anxiety

"Personally, Matt, I think you suffer from acute castration anxiety so you fantasize that all women are murderers."
> —Kimberly playing shrink in "In-Laws and Outlaws," 1994

On the World of Modeling

"I am not a piece of meat."
> —Jake rejecting the modeling profession in "Hot and Bothered," 1993

"I'm a model. I starve so that others may drool."
> —A witty fashion model to Jo in "Carpe Diem," 1993

"Let me explain how modeling works. You are fawned over, fussed with, made to look good for the camera. That is what your body was hired for. It's the nature of the beast."
> —Amanda addresses Jake's concerns in "Hot and Bothered," 1993

On the Importance of Regular Exercise

"I'm living proof that someone can eat whatever they want and never exercise and still look absolutely gorgeous."
> —Sandy's true confession in "Leap of Faith," 1992

On Kinkiness

"That I can touch my nose with my tongue."
> —Andrew Shue on his kinkiest fetish, quoted in *Vanity Fair*, 1993

On the Appeal of Male Sensitivity

"I hate that sensitive man thing. Come on, where's the rat I love?"
> —Kimberly to Michael shortly before their accident in "Collision Course," 1993

Timothy White

On Big Misunderstandings

"Syd's not bad. She's just misunderstood."
> —Laura Leighton defending her character, quoted in *Rolling Stone*, 1994

"Amanda's really misunderstood."
> —Heather Locklear, quoted in *Rolling Stone*, 1994

On the Perils of the Medical Profession

"I've seen so many people turned inside out, I have trouble looking at people without seeing their internal organs."
> —Michael opening up in the pilot episode, 1992

"I'm not some bimbo. I'm a doctor for God's sake."
—Kimberly complaining to Michael about being overqualified to be
the other woman in "Pas de Trois," 1993

"You're kind of arrogant, even for a surgeon."
—Amanda realizing Dr. Peter Burns may have a few flaws in
"The Cook, the Creep, His Lover, and Her Sister," 1994

On the Proper Bedside Manner

"Where'd you go to nursing school—Guantanemo?"
—Dr. Mancini criticizing a nurse in "Under the Mistletoe," 1993

*"No wonder your red count was so off—you don't have blood in your
veins, you have snake venom."*
—Michael's diagnosis of Amanda in
"Hose by Any Other Name," 1995

On Memorable Pickup Lines

"You can tell a lot about people by the way they pack their lunches."
—Rick, the idea-stealing sun screen heir/mailroom boy at D&D,
sweet-talking Alison in "For Love or Money," 1992

*"Just the two of us spending a nice quiet night at your place making
it together . . . the lasagna, I meant."*
—Kelly Taylor talking dirty to Jake in the supermarket as
she describes her lusty hopes for their evening in
"Lost and Found," 1992

"Talk to him about the plight of the sea otter."
—Matt suggesting a conversation starter for Alison to
say to her new environmentally concerned love interest Keith in
"Polluted Affair," 1992

"How do you look in this?"
—Alison's loaded question to Keith as she hands him a condom
(which Billy had given her) before they make love for the first time
in "Polluted Affair," 1992

Wayne Stambler

"Take off your pants, doctor."
—Jane hits on her husband in "Jake Versus Jake," 1992

JO: *This is a nice shirt, but it'll look better on the floor.*
JAKE: *That goes double for you.*
—Jo and Jake talking dirty before their first time together in "Three's a Crowd," 1993

"Alison, it's okay to be beautiful."
—Alison's psychiatrist Dr. Daniel Miller offering his professional opinion in "Psycho-Therapy," 1994

"So how did someone as beautiful as you not become a model?"
—Future business associate and perverted ripoff artist–psycho Chris Marchette pitching woo to Jane in "Till Death Do Us Part," 1994

On Failures of the Freudian Approach

"What do you do with your tough cases—what do you do, take them to Club Med?"
—Billy questioning Alison's psychiatrist in "Psycho-Therapy," 1994

On Safe Sex Seductions

"I've wanted to be with you for so long. I hope this doesn't sound too forward, but I've got a condom in my purse."
> —Jane getting to the point with her freaky but reluctant Aussie paramour, Chris, in "No Strings Attached," 1994

On Southern Charms

BILLY: *I miss your smile.*
ALISON: *Yeah, I miss a lot of things too.*
BILLY: *For instance?*
ALISON: *Your smile, your lips, and everything south.*
> —Young love reheating one more time in New York City in "Swept Away," 1994

On the World's Oldest Profession

SYDNEY: *You arrange sex dates for a living?*
LAUREN: *Oh, that's a quaint way of putting it.*
> —Sydney gets a clue about her new job pressing the flesh from her boss in "Collision Course," 1993

"Boy, you don't miss a trick, do ya. Sorry, bad choice of words."
> —Michael ribbing Sydney on her career choices in "Young Men and the Sea," 1994

On Stating the Obvious

"I have news for you. I'm not perfect."
> —Michael makes a big confession to Jane in "Burned," 1992

On Modest Proposals

"Can you think of two people who deserve each other more?"
> —Kimberly to Michael before their Las Vegas nuptials in "Love Reeks," 1994

On the Pacific Northwest

"Alison, don't forget your raincoat."
—Amanda's concerned advice to Alison who's moving to Seattle in
"Irreconcilable Similarities," 1993

On Birds of a Feather Flocking

"I think Jane might have been right about us. Ozzie and Harriet we ain't, but we do belong together."
—Michael recognizing Sydney as a kindred spirit in
"Psycho-Therapy," 1994

On Absence Making the Heart Grow Fonder

BILLY: *Oh, I miss you.*
ALISON: *I miss you too.*
—A sentiment these two will express many times in the future,
shared possibly for the first time after she returns for the funeral of
Billy's father in "End Game," 1993

On Playing Hardball

JANE: *You're scum, Michael.*
MICHAEL: *Well, you know, you play hardball with me and I'm going to knock it out of the park every time.*
—A triumphant Michael takes time to gloat to his ex-wife in
"Dr. Jeckyl Saves His Hide," 1994

On Phone Sex

BILLY: *So what are you wearing?*
ALISON: *Billy!*
BILLY: *Just curious.*
ALISON: *Is this what I've been reduced to—phone sex?*
BILLY: *Well, we are on opposite sides of the country. What are the alternatives?*

ALISON: *That's pretty cynical.*
BILLY: *No, just practical.*
—The young love birds discovering the realities of long-distance
love in "Parting Glances," 1994

On the Plight of the American Farmer

*"Alison, you're a wholesome woman. . . . Some men, they get turned
on by that—well, like farmers and the 4-H crowd."*
—Billy's curious compliment in "Pas de Trois," 1993

On Glasnost

MATT: *This isn't Russia. The walls don't have ears. There's no KGB
lurking in the shadows.*
KATYA: *For your information, there no longer exists the KGB in Russia. It only lives in stupid American films.*
—The newly married couple grapple with the post–Cold War
changes in "Married to It," 1993

On Illegal Immigration

*"Look, Matt, I like you. But personally I do question the ethics and
legality of this whole situation. The country is having a tough enough
time taking care of its own, if you know what I mean."*
—Amanda explaining why she won't back up his lies to the
immigration man regarding his faux marriage to Katya in
"Married to It," 1994

On Words of Comfort

MICHAEL: *Before you blow a gasket, Amanda's in I.C.U. She may not
make it.*
KIMBERLY: *So she willed you her Wonder Bra?*
—A jealous Kimberly kicking an ailing Amanda while she's down in
"To Live and Die in Malibu," 1995

On the Appeal of Rock Stars

"She's just so, so straight, and a little shy herself and it just gives her life a little edge I think."

—Heather Locklear's mother, in an interview
with Barbara Walters, 1994

On the Need for Space

"Everybody in our building is too damn concerned with everyone's business."

—Michael making a breakthrough over drinks at Shooters
with Billy in "Pas de Trois," 1993

On Deception

"This is incredible—the woman who wrote the Cliff Notes for How to Lie Your Ass Off, *and you believe her?"*

—Michael calling Sydney's truthfulness into question in
"Breakfast at Tiffany's, Dinner at Eight," 1995

On Puritanism

"I don't deal in tramps!"

—Hollywood madam Lauren's curious putdown of Sydney in
"Devil with the G-String On," 1994

On Big Comebacks

KIMBERLY: *Rumors of my death, as they say, were premature.*
MICHAEL: *You were dead! Your mother said you were dead. She called the hospital.*
KIMBERLY: *I know she always was a bit controlling, but that's over-stepping it a little, don't you think.*

—Kimberly's and Michael's touching reunion in
"The Bitch Is Back," 1994

On the Necessity of Prioritizing

"Maybe I didn't make myself clear last night. I've come back to claim what's mine, and you're the first thing on my list."
— Kimberly getting things straight with Michael in "The Bitch Is Back," 1994

On Getting a Second Medical Opinion

KIMBERLY: *Listen you opportunistic little bitch, if you think that shotgun marriage you arranged is going to protect you, then you're dumber than you look. Now stay out of our lives and you won't get hurt, okay?*
SYDNEY: *What—am I supposed to be afraid of? You?*
KIMBERLY: *My professional opinion—you bet your ass.*
— The women in Michael's life trying to sort things out in "The Bitch Is Back," 1994

On Ghosts

"You're impossible. Even dead, you're impossible."
— Jo complaining to Reed, the departed but-not-dear father of her child in "Love, Mancini Style," 1994

On Gravity

"Finally, the reaction I've been looking for."
— Kimberly's comment after Sydney faints when she sees Kim alive and well in "The Bitch Is Back," 1994

Dan Cortese as Jess.

Doug Hyun

On Being Indiscreet

"I thought you might want to know that Jess and Jo were in her darkroom all night developing more than head shots."
>—Sydney tattling to Jake about his brother's and Jo's after-hours activities in "Hose by Any Other Name," 1995

On Sibling Rivalry

JANE: *Gram loved you. She tried hard to reach out to you.*
SYDNEY: *Well, I guess her arms weren't long enough to reach past you.*
>—A warm, sisterly moment from "The Two Mrs. Mancinis," 1994

On Management Skills

"Well, it's payback time. I promise to make your life a living hell, and I always keep my promises. Oh, and don't even bother quitting. With the report I can put in your personnel file, you wouldn't get a job bagging groceries."
>—Amanda giving Alison one of her periodic informal performance reviews in "Grand Delusions," 1994

On Things Never Being What They Seem

"Don't worry, you're safe now."
>—Alison's psycho-love interest Keith comforting her about being stalked by . . . well, by him, in "Suspicious Minds," 1993

On the Power of Positive Thinking

"I think I'm really gonna love it here."
>—Amanda on moving into her new property at *Melrose Place*

On Crime and Punishment

"Look, bitch, just kill me or call the cops, all right? The martyr routine is getting old."
>—Ted the peeping handyman requesting a fair and speedy trial from Amanda in "Psycho-Therapy," 1994

On Male Bonding

"Go to hell you son of a bitch."
—Jake's negative response to Billy's request that he be his best man at his wedding to Alison. Jake's declining the invitation preceded him punching Billy in the face in "With This Ball and Chain," 1994

On the Concept of Love at First Sight

"It wasn't like I looked at him and went, 'Ding! Ding! Ding!' It was just something that evolved."
—Laura Leighton addressing the start of her romance with Grant Show, quoted in *Us* magazine, 1994

On the Dangers of Being Judgmental

"Everything's so black and white with you, isn't it? That's why you're a loser and you always will be for the rest of your life."
—Amanda's constructive criticism to Jake in "Till Death Do Us Part," 1994

On Whether Michael Is Great in Bed

"God, I never really thought about it like that."
—Josie Bissett, 1994

KIMBERLY: *God, Michael, it hasn't been like that since. . . . Come to think of it, I don't think it's ever been like that.*
MICHAEL: *That's a good thing, right?*
KIMBERLY: *Good, I give you a nine point nine, with bonus points for difficulty.*
—Some after-sex chit-chat with an ocean view from "Grand Delusions," 1994

"Michael may be an ass, but at least he can do it."
—Jane putting down her coy fiancé, Chris, in "Love Reeks," 1994

On Michael as God's Gift to Women

JAKE: *You may not be God's gift, but you sure are God's revenge on women.*
MICHAEL: *Yeah, I guess I am.*
—A male-bonding moment of truth from "Reunion Blues," 1994

On Truthfulness in Advertising

BRUCE: *Attractive, intelligent-looking, upscale. Who are they?*
AMANDA: *The Doctors Frankenstein.*
—Amanda's boss trying to recruit Michael and Kimberly to appear in a Factor's Gourmet Coffee ad in "The Cook, the Creep, His Lover, and Her Sister," 1994

On Fun Couples

"All I can say is thank God you didn't have children."
—Wilshire Memorial's chief of staff, Roy Hobbs, to Michael and Kimberly in "Kiss Kiss Bang Bang," 1995

On Unlikely Couples

ALISON: *It's funny, you and me. We would never have been friends in high school.*
JAKE: *It's 'cause nice girls like you never gave me the time of day.*
ALISON: *Tough guys like you never asked.*
—Preliminary chat before Alison and Jake kiss for the first time in their brief, mostly off-screen fling in "Second Chances," 1992

On the Whore/Madonna Complex

"Sydney, everything's going to work out for the two of us. You'll see. I've decided to marry Jane. That'll make me your brother-in-law. Then I'll have everything I've ever wanted—a mother for my children and a whore just for me."
—Jane's creepy fiancé, Chris Marchette, reaching out to her sister in "The Cook, the Creep, His Lover, and Her Sister," 1994

SYDNEY: *Why are you doing this? You're supposed to be in love with my sister.*
CHRIS: *Jane lacks that slutty quality that you have in spades.*
—Chris explaining his motives in "The Days of Wine and Vodka," 1994

On the Ideal Man

"He is amazing, Billy. Committed, intelligent, sweet, full of integrity . . . great butt."
—Alison explains the attributes of Keith—who it turns out ought to be committed—to Billy in "Polluted Affair," 1992

On Police Harassment

DETECTIVE JOHN RAWLINGS: *I set her straight. You let me know if she steps out of bounds again.*
MATT: *This is police harassment you're talking about.*
DETECTIVE JOHN RAWLINGS: *I prefer to think of it as a perk.*
—Matt questioning his obsessive officer's use of extreme force with Kimberly in "Boxing Sydney," 1995

On Alcoholism

"It's not even lunch time and you're already into happy hour."
—A concerned Amanda cautions Alison on her drinking in "Just Say No," 1994

On Sobriety

BILLY: *You're drunk.*
ALISON: *Yeah, well you're a self-centered pig. At least in the morning, I'll be sober.*
—Even stewed, Alison manages to paraphrase a Winston Churchill putdown in "Dr. Jeckyl Saves His Hide," 1994

On Capitalism

REED: *Amanda's rich?*
JO: *Yeah, in a capitalist, greedy, screwing-everyone-else kind of way.*
>—Jo and her psychotic, drug-dealing love interest discuss microeconomics in "Arousing Suspicion," 1994

On the Battle Between the Sexes

BILLY: *They're yang and we're yin.*
MATT: *Billy, I think it's the other way around.*
>—A drunken male-bonding conversation about women from "Leap of Faith," 1992

On Inheritance

"Perfect timing, Syd. Come to pay your respects to Gram's money?"
>—Jane's reaction to her sister's last-minute appearance at the reading of their grandmother's will in "The Two Mrs. Mancinis," 1994

On Slackers

"Cut me a little slack. It's just not fair. The day I graduated the whole economy went in the toilet."
>—Billy justifying his defaulting on his student loan in "Polluted Affair," 1992

On Mercy Killings

KIMBERLY: *He's a menace, Sydney, that must be contained.*
SYDNEY: *What can we do?*
KIMBERLY: *Same thing you do to a rabid dog. Put him out of his misery.*
SYDNEY: *You mean murder?*
KIMBERLY: *No, I mean justice.*
>—Kim and Syd talk about washing that man right out of their hair in "Till Death Do Us Part," 1994

Wayne Stambler

On Methodology

SYDNEY: *How about the old blow dryer in the bathtub routine?*
KIMBERLY: *Michael never takes baths. Besides, it's more than likely that the fuse would blow before he actually fries.*
　　—Syd and Kim brainstorm about how to improve matters with Michael in "Till Death Do Us Part," 1994

On Kidnapping

"You know, for a kidnapping victim you look pretty good. Where'd you get those diamonds?"
　　—Jake saving the day for Sydney—sort of—in "Just Say No," 1994

On Blond Ambition

KIMBERLY: *What's she doing here?*
MICHAEL: *She's my patient.*
KIMBERLY: *What's wrong, peroxide poisoning?*
　　—The young lovers discussing Michael's new patient Amanda in "Boxing Sydney," 1995

"What's it going to be, Michael? Cold hard cash or a bleached blond with dark roots?"
　　—Kimberly forcing Michael to decide between her and Amanda in "To Live and Die in Malibu," 1995

On Michael's Feelings for Jane

"I just hate to see her happy."
　　—Michael explaining his feelings about his ex-wife to future-wife Sydney in "No Bed of Roses," 1993

On Entomology

"I never really pictured Amanda as the social butterfly type. A social moth maybe. A black widow, definitely."
> —Alison speaking well of her new landlord in "Much Ado About Everything," 1993

On Paraphrasing

"What's that old expression? If you don't have anything nice to say, then shut your mouth."
> —Alison misquoting slightly to Billy in "Drawing the Line," 1992

On Greeting Cards

ALISON: *Life doesn't always come neatly packaged, and neither does love.*
BILLY: *You should listen to yourself. You sound like a dysfunctional Hallmark card.*
> —A tense moment during the Keith affair in "Drawing the Line," 1992

On Sydney Versus Amanda

"Who's scarier, Sydney or Amanda? I guess I'd have to say Sydney because she's a psychotic."
> —Grant Show making a tough call, quoted in *Rolling Stone*, 1994

On Brotherhood

JESS: *I walk out that door, Jake, and that's it. I don't have a brother.*
JAKE: *It works for me.*
> —A tense moment of sibling rivalry in "The Big Bang Theory," 1995

On Sex and Violence

MATT: *Don't you ever touch me again.*
MICHAEL: *When's the last time you said that to a guy? Huh, Matt?*
MATT: *Go to hell, Michael.*
—Matt and Michael have harsh words before Matt decks the doctor in "The Two Mrs. Mancinis," 1994

On Sex Addiction

"I was up all night thinking. You're a sex maniac. Did you just fall off the wagon?"
—Alison's worried pillow talk after scoring with her sex addict football star boyfriend Terry in "Bye-Bye Baby," 1995

Diego Uchitel

On the Moral Decline of Our Society

"All I can say is that you guys are all a bunch of degenerates."
—Billy addressing everyone attending his bachelor party in "Devil with the G-String On," 1994

On the Absurdity of Contemporary Life

"Boy, things are sure getting weird around here."
—Jane considers all the *Melrose* madness in "Till Death Do Us Part," 1994

179

Future Shock

Nobody—not even Aaron Spelling—knows exactly what's going to happen on *Melrose Place* from week to week, much less decade to decade. And so the reader should keep in mind that the following off-the-cuff comments are nothing more than informed guesses about what the future might hold for *Melrose*'s wild bunch around the time they all become middle-aged—in other words, just in time for a *Melrose* reunion special.

See you there.

Heather Locklear on Amanda:

"Amanda will be the same, but will visit the beauty salon more often—to cover her roots."

Daphne Zuniga on Jo:

"Jo will be like Norma Desmond, only her mansion will be filled with beautiful house boys."

Grant Show on Jake:

"He'll be drowned, I think. He'll be dead. I don't think he'll make it.

At the reunion, people will be asking where he's at. Maybe it'll be a big mystery."

Laura Leighton on Syd:

"Anything is possible with Syd."

Andrew Shue on Billy:

"Billy at fifty will either be off writing in some remote place, like a log cabin writing short stories, or he'll be a powerful journalist like Jann Wenner."

Courtney Thorne-Smith on Alison:

"If she doesn't get some very comprehensive therapy, she'll be doing the exact same thing. She's just the queen of doing the same thing but expecting different results. Absolute insanity."

Doug Savant on Matt:

"I see Matt at fifty independently wealthy, living with his lover on a wide-open ranch in Montana. Somehow he's broken free of the building. I don't know how he gets back for the reunion show, but somehow he's dragged back in."

Marcia Cross on Kimberly:

"I think the fun thing about Kim is that you don't know if this woman is going to wind up being a nun in a convent, a stripper in some sleazy bar, or a major medical research genius. That's what I love about her."

Aaron Spelling on Amanda:

"I think Amanda will be the same. She's slept with everyone, and she's going to find out that life is not sex. I think she'll eventually meet someone she loves very much and have the personification of a perfect love affair. She'll have a child just as beautiful as Amanda, and I think that child will be doing a series for me."

Aaron Spelling on Billy and Alison:

"I think they'll be a little like Don Johnson and Melanie Griffith. I think they'll break up and make up and break up and make up. I see them being married at least three times."

Aaron Spelling on Matt:

"I don't think we've met the guy Matt is going to marry. But I hope he's someone who'll care about Matt as much as Matt will care about him. They'll adopt a child and be the best parents you've ever seen. It'll be the most romantic marriage. He'll invite his parents, but they probably won't come."

Aaron Spelling on Jo:

"I think Jo will eventually turn out to be Annie Leibovitz of her time. I don't think she'll ever get married for some reason."

Aaron Spelling on Jake:

"By the time of the reunion, he'll be racing cars. I think he'll get a fixation on what Paul Newman did. I think he'll be killed in a fiery crash just trying to push it."

Aaron Spelling on Sydney:

"I think Sydney will become a nun. I really do. She's been every-where, had everybody. She's destroyed lives, and I think she'll spend the rest of her life trying to compensate."

Aaron Spelling on Jane:

"I think poor Jane is doomed to horrible relationships. I think she wears her vulnerability on her sleeve—she's a canary with a broken wing who flies to anyone who says, 'I care about you.' At the reunion, Jane would probably be the one who commits suicide."

Aaron Spelling on Michael:

"I think he'll have a nervous breakdown. He'll spend about five years in an institution and be confused about whether he's Jake or Matt or Billy or all of them. Then I think he'll come out of it and probably become a lawyer."

About the Author

David Wild is a senior editor at *Rolling Stone*. He is a 1984 graduate of Cornell University. He and his wife, Fran, live in Los Angeles, within walking distance of Melrose Place.